D0842503

THE
INDEX
REVOLUTION

THE
INDEX
REVOLUTION

Why Investors Should Join It Now

Charles D. Ellis

WILEY

Published by John Wiley & Sons, Inc., Hoboken, New Jersey.

Published simultaneously in Canada.

For general information on our other products and services or for technical support, please contact our Customer Care Department within the United States at (800) 762-2974, outside the United States at (317) 572-3993 or fax (317) 572-4002.

Wiley publishes in a variety of print and electronic formats and by print-on-demand. Some material included with standard print versions of this book may not be included in e-books or in print-on-demand. If this book refers to media such as a CD or DVD that is not included in the version you purchased, you may download this material at http://booksupport.wiley.com. For more information about Wiley products, visit www.wiley.com.

Library of Congress Cataloging-in-Publication Data:

ISBN 9781119313076 (Hardcover)
ISBN 9781119313090 (ePDF)
ISBN 9781119313083 (ePub)

Printed in the United States of America

CONTENTS

Contents

FOREWORD

As a person who has believed in indexing all my life, I am delighted to add my voice in support of the important message of this book. *The Index Revolution* is not only a history of the growth of indexing over the past 40 years, but also a call to those who may have been slow to accept this revolutionary method of portfolio management. If you are still attracted to high-expense, actively managed mutual funds (or, worse, if you have chosen to invest in hedge funds), Charley Ellis's succinct arguments as well as his marvelous anecdotes should leave no lingering doubts in your mind: index investing represents a superior investment strategy, and everyone should use index funds as the core of their investment portfolios.

Every year, mutual-fund advertisements proudly declare that "this year will be a stock-pickers' market."

They may admit that during the previous year it was all right to be invested in a simple index fund, but they say that the value of professional investment management will become apparent in the current year. *Barron's* ran a cover story in 2015 and made the same case in 2016 that "active" portfolio managers would "recapture their lost glory." In early 2014 The *Wall Street Journal* ran an article predicting that 2014 would be a stock-pickers' market. Money managers have a number of clichés they use to promote their high-priced services, and "stock-pickers' market" is one of their favorites. But year after year, when the results come in, low-cost index funds prove their worth as the optimal way to invest.

Indexing outperforms in both bull and bear markets. Active management will not protect you by moving out of stocks when markets decline. No one can consistently time the market. There is no evidence to support the claim that active managers do better when there is more or less dispersion in the returns for individual stocks. Nor is it the case that indexing does worse during periods of rising interest rates. While in every year there will always be some actively managed funds that beat the market, the odds of your finding one are stacked against you. And there is little persistence in mutual fund returns. The fact that a fund is an outperformer in one year is no guarantee that it will be a winner in the next. Indeed, Morningstar, the mutual fund rating company, found that its ratings, based on past performance, were not useful in predicting future returns. Their five-star-rated funds, the top performers, actually did worse over the next year than the lowest one-star-rated Morningstar Funds.

Morningstar found that the only variable that was reliably correlated with the next year's performance was the fund's expense ratio. Funds with low expense ratios and low turnover tend to outperform funds with high turnover and high expenses (even before considering the adverse tax effects of high-turnover funds). Of course, the quintessential low-turnover, low-expense funds are index funds, which simply buy and hold all the stocks in a particular market and do not trade from stock to stock.

Standard & Poor's Dow Jones Indices published a statistical analysis in 2016 detailing the dismal record of "active" portfolio managers: As is typically the case, about two-thirds of active large-capitalization managers underperformed the S&P 500 large-cap index during 2015. Nor were managers any better in the supposedly less efficient, small-capitalization universe. Almost three-quarters of small-cap managers underperformed the S&P

Small-Cap Index. When S&P measured performance over a longer time period, the results got worse. Over 80 percent of large-cap managers and almost 90 percent of small-cap managers underperformed their benchmark indexes over a ten-year period through December 2015.

The same findings have been documented in international markets. Even in the less efficient emerging markets, index funds regularly outperform active funds. The very inefficiency of emerging markets (including large bid-asked spreads, market impact costs, and a variety of stamp taxes on transactions) makes the strategy of simply buying and holding a broad indexed portfolio an optimal strategy in these markets, too. And indexing has proved its merit in the bond markets as well. The high-yield bond market is often considered to be best accessed via active investing, as passive vehicles have structural constraints that limit their flexibility and ability to deal with credit risk. Nevertheless, Standard & Poor's found that the 10-year results through 2015 for the actively managed high-yield funds category show that over 90 percent of funds underperformed their broad-based benchmarks.

It is true that in every period there are some managers who do outperform. But there is little consistency. The best managers in one period are usually not the same as the outperformers in the next. And even celebrity managers like William Miller, who racked up market-beating returns over a decade, underperformed over the next several years. Your chances of picking the best managers for the next decade are virtually nil. You are far more likely to end up with a typical underperforming, high-priced manager who will produce returns for you that are lower than index returns by an amount about equal to the difference in the fees that are charged. Buying a low-cost index fund or exchange-traded fund (ETF) is the superior investment strategy. Trying to predict the next star manager is, in Charley Ellis's famous words, "a loser's game."

Do you want more proof? In this slim volume, Charley presents a compendium of dismal results showing the futility of trying to beat the market. He also presents a number of additional arguments for indexing such as its simplicity and tax efficiency. And if you don't believe me or even Charley, remember that Warren Buffett, perhaps the greatest investor of our time, has opined that all investors would be better off if their portfolio contained a diversified group of index funds.

In this readable volume, Charley describes how indexing was originally thought to be an inferior way to invest and even "un-American." But as time went on and the evidence became stronger and stronger, the case for indexing became air tight. Indeed, the Ellis thesis, brilliantly explained in these pages, is that changes in the structure of the stock market now make it virtually impossible for money managers to outperform the market. Perhaps 50 years ago when our stock markets were dominated by individual investors, professionals, who visited companies to talk with management and were the first to know about company prospects, might have been able to select the best stocks and beat the market. But now we have fair disclosure regulations that require companies to make public announcements of any material facts that could influence their share price. And perhaps 98 percent of the trading is done by professionals with equally superb information and technology rather than by individuals. The irony is that in such an environment it is increasingly difficult for any professional to beat the market by enough to cover the extra fees and costs involved in trying.

The Index Revolution is not only a historical explanation of the growing acceptance of indexing over the past 50 years, but also an account of the personal evolution of a former believer in active management. Charley Ellis began his career as a firm believer in the usefulness of

traditional security analysis and the potential superiority of professional management of common stock portfolios. He founded the firm Greenwich Associates that
provides advisory services to the financial industry, and
particularly to major investment managers. As a firsthand
participant in the growth of the industry, Charley was in
the perfect position to understand how vast changes in
the environment made the traditional services of active
portfolio managers increasingly less effective.

The paradox of security analysis and active stock selection is that as their practitioners become more professional and skilled, markets become more efficient and the
search for mispriced securities becomes increasingly more
difficult. Whenever information now becomes available
about an industry or an individual stock, it gets reflected
in the prices of individual stocks without delay. That
does not mean that prices are always "correct." Indeed,
we know *after* the fact that prices are frequently "wrong."
But at any point in time, no one knows for sure whether
they are too high or too low. And betting against the collective wisdom of many thousands of professional market
participants is likely to be a "loser's game." Correct perceptions of mispricing are no more likely than incorrect
perceptions, and active management adds considerable

costs to the process as well as being extremely tax inefficient for taxable investors.

When Vanguard launched the first index, its chairman, John Bogle, hoped to raise $150 million in the fund's initial public offering. In fact, only $11.4 million was raised, and the new fund was called "Bogle's Folly." The fund grew only slowly over the next several years and was denigrated by professional investment advisers and dismissed as "settling for mediocrity." But experience was the best teacher. Investors came to realize that index investing was superior investing, and index funds with their low fees regularly outperformed actively managed funds. And index funds grew steadily over time.

Today, indexed mutual funds have over $2 trillion of investment assets. And exchange-traded (index) funds have approximately the same amount of assets. According to Morningstar, during 2015 investors pulled over $200 billion out of actively managed funds while they were pouring over $400 billion into index funds. These shifts are the latest evidence of a sea change in the asset management business. The index revolution is real, and the winners are individual and institutional investors who understand the superiority of indexing.

While indexing has grown sharply over the years, it still represents only about 30 percent of the total investment dollars. So the revolution still has lots of room to grow. Why so many investors continue to pay for expensive portfolio management advice of questionable value is testimony to the power of hope over experience. But, as Albert Einstein has taught us, "Insanity (is) doing the same thing over and over again and expecting different results."

It is very clear that the core of every investment portfolio and certainly the composition of every retirement portfolio should be invested in low-cost index funds. If you are not convinced, and if you would like an expert like Charley Ellis to convince you that indexing is the optimal investment strategy, read this wonderful little book. It will be the most financially rewarding two hours you could possibly spend.

Burton G. Malkiel
Princeton

INTRODUCTION

At the risk of "removing the punch bowl just when the party was really warming up"[1] or offending my many friends among active managers, the purpose of this book is to show investors how much the world of investing has changed—changed so much and in so many compounding ways—that the skills and concepts of "performance" investing no longer work. In a profound irony, the collective excellence of active professional investors has made it almost impossible for almost any of them to succeed—after fees and costs—at beating the market. So investors need to know how much the world of investing has changed and what they can do now to achieve investing success.

While 50 years ago active investors could realistically aim to outperform the market, often by substantial margins, major basic changes have combined to make it unrealistic to try to beat today's market—the consensus of many experts, all working with equally superb information and technology—by enough to justify paying the fees and costs of trying. For investment implementation, the time has come to switch to low-cost index funds and exchange-traded funds (ETFs).

Investors now can—and we all certainly should—use the time liberated by that switch to focus on important long-term investment questions that center on knowing who we really are as investors. We should start by defining our true and realistic long-term investment goals, recognizing that each of us has a unique combination of income, assets, time, responsibilities, experiences, expertise, interest in investing, and so on. Then, with a realistic understanding of the long-term *and* short-term nature of the capital markets, we can each design realistic investment policies that will enable us to enjoy long-term investment success. This is important work and should be Priority One for every investor.

All investors, whether individuals or institutions, should decide carefully whether to move away from conventional "beat the market" active investing. There are three compelling reasons to do this. First, indexing reliably delivers better long-term returns (as will be documented in Part Two, Chapter 2). Second, indexing is much cheaper and incurs less in taxes for individuals. In today's professional market, such "small" differences make a big difference. Third, indexing frees us from the micro complexities of active investing so we can focus our time and attention on the *macro* decisions that are really important.

I hope that many remarkably capable and hardworking investment professionals will find this short book a "wake-up call" to redefine their responsibilities and the real purpose of their work. Many years ago, investment managers used to balance their intense focus on *price discovery* (beating the market by exploiting the mistakes of other investors) with at least equal emphasis on *value discovery* (helping clients think through and define their unique long-term objectives) and then would design for each client those long-term investment policy commitments most capable of achieving the long-term objectives. Because such customized professional counseling service "doesn't scale," while a focus on standardized investment products does scale and can produce a superbly profitable business, most investment managers have increasingly emphasized products. It's time to "rebalance." First, most investors can use professional help in determining optimal investment policies. Second, the old "beat the market" mantra is out of date and out of touch with today's reality.

The world's active managers are now so good and compete so vigorously to excel that almost none of them can expect—after fees and costs—to beat the consensus of all the other experts on price discovery. As hard data now show, over the long term the markets have gone through such extraordinary changes that it's no longer worth the fees, costs, and risks of trying to beat them. That's why the old money game is over.

The phenomenal half-century transformation of the securities markets and investment management have been caused by an amazing influx of talent, information, expertise, and technology—and increasingly high fees. As a result, the central proposition of active investing, which worked so well many years ago, has gone through a classic bell curve and become an almost certain loser's game. (A loser's game is a contest—like club tennis—in which the win-lose outcome is determined not by the successes of the winner, but by the mistakes and failures of the loser.)

Active investing, as now practiced by most mutual funds and most managers of pension and endowment funds, typically involves portfolios with 60 to 80 different stocks and annual turnover of 60 to 100 percent. As will be shown in Part Two, Chapter 2, more than 98 percent of all stock market trading is now done by professional investors or computer algorithms. Active investors are almost always buying from or selling to expert professionals who are part of a superb global information network and are very hard to beat.

Even in today's highly efficient markets, a few exceptional investment managers* may outperform the market after fees, costs, and taxes. Many more will *believe* they can—or will *say* they can—than will ever succeed. And even for the few who succeed over the long term, the magnitude of their better performance will be small. To make matters worse for investors, there is no known way to identify the exceptional few in advance. What's more, investors need to know that the "data" on past performance, sadly, are all too often distorted and so are seriously misleading.

---

* Most of the exceptions will be small firms that are hard to identify and are particularly likely to change. Among the major firms, three exceptions appear to be Vanguard, with its emphasis on low fees, indexing, and careful selection of external active managers; and Capital Group and T. Rowe Price, with their equal focus on proprietary research and strong cultures centered on long-term values and discipline.

Fortunately, neither individual nor institutional investors have to play the loser's game of active investing. By indexing investment operations at very low cost and accepting that active professionals have set securities prices about as correctly as is possible, index investors know that over the long term, they will achieve better results than other investors, particularly those who stay with active investing—the once promising approach that is now out of date and, with few exceptions, doomed to disappoint.

Part One of this book explains my personal half-century odyssey from confident enthusiasm for active investing through increasing doubt as the market changed and changed again, culminating in my slow arrival at the now self-evident conclusion: The major stock markets have changed so much and fees and costs are now so important that almost all investors will be wise to change to low-cost indexing for implementation and concentrate where each client is unique and decisions really matter: investment policy.

In Part Two, you will find 10 good reasons most investors, both individuals and institutions, will be wise to index now or, at the very least, give indexing careful consideration. The first 4 are the major, undeniable reasons.

The next 6 reasons are important, too. Here, briefly, are the reasons that will then be explained, each in its own chapter.

1. Over the past half-century, the major stock markets have changed so greatly—in so many important ways—that beating the market regularly has become much, much harder, making indexing more and more sensible for all investors. While the U.S. stock market is our focus, comparably major changes have occurred in all major stock markets around the world.

2. Indexing earns higher rates of return. A large majority of actively managed funds underperform index funds—particularly when hidden failed funds are included in the data for historical accuracy. In a largely random distribution, some managers do outperform, but there's no known way to identify the future winners in advance. The proportion of active managers that underperform after costs and fees will vary from year to year, but the longer the period of evaluation, the larger the proportion falling short.

3. Low fees are an important reason to index. High fees are the main and most persistent reason active funds underperform low-cost index funds.

4. Indexing makes it much easier to focus on your most important *strategic* investment decisions—correctly centered on you, your objectives, and your resources—where you and your adviser can make a major, positive difference to your long-term success as an investor.

5. Your taxes are lower when you index.

6. Indexing saves money on trading operations and makes most investment risks easier to live with.

7. Indexing avoids serious manager risks and reduces the need to change from manager to manager. Both are costly to investors.

8. Indexing helps you avoid costly troubles with that rascal troublemaker Mr. Market, a gyrating gigolo who represents the temptations of market trading.

9. You have much better things to do with your time and energy.

10. Experts on investing agree that most investors should index.

When all these reasons are combined, they make a compelling case for accepting reality and indexing *now*.

NINE SILLY "REASONS" NOT TO INDEX

Now that you know the 10 good reasons to index, let's briefly consider nine candidly silly reasons you may sometimes hear *not* to index. Beware: People will say the darnedest things to defend an idea they have been believing for some time that somehow *feels* "right" to them even when they have little or no solid supporting evidence—particularly people whose high incomes depend on it.

Here are some "reasons" that you may hear—with a brief explanation of why each does not make sense.

1. *"Indexing is for losers—people who will accept being mediocre or just average."* The record shows that index investors' results are better. The success secret of all great investors is rational decision making based on objective information. This book documents the compelling record of low-cost indexing and explains why indexing works better than conventional active or performance investing.

2. *"Passive is no way to succeed at anything. Why assume you can't do better? Why give up trying?"* Einstein is said to have explained insanity as doing the same thing again and again while hoping for a different outcome. Active investing, as the record shows, no longer works. Indexing works better for many good, fact-based reasons.

3. *"Indexing forces investors to buy overpriced stocks and then ride them down."* Equally, indexing "forces" investors to buy underpriced stocks and ride them up. Long-term investors know that many "overpriced" stocks of the past have gone on to much higher prices as their growth in earnings exceeded expectations.

4. *"With indexing, you let a small group of unknown clerks select your stocks."* Knowing the individuals' names is not important, but we do know that the major index creators such as S&P Dow Jones, and FTSE select index technicians carefully. Their corporate reputations depend on careful adjustments being consistently made to the stocks in each index and they know many people are always looking.

5. *"Maybe next year I'll index. I'm too busy to index now."* Indexing can be done in less than half an hour. No need to rush, of course, but why wait and continue to incur all the costs and risks of active investing?

6. *"With the stock market at a high level, this is not the right time to switch to indexing."* Many investors assume active managers outperform in down markets for two reasons: The fund manager can go into cash or the fund manager can shift to defensive stocks. But in practice this has not happened any more often than would be expected from random numbers.

7. *"Instead of 'market capitalization' index funds, I'm going with 'smart beta' funds."* Please start with Appendix A, on smart beta, and be sure any manager you might consider who adjusts "market cap" indexes for such "fundamental" factors as value or momentum has a long track record of success as an investment manager, not just as a sales organization.

8. *"Active funds beat index funds last year. They are coming back!"* Some years, a majority of actively managed funds outperform index funds, as

shown in Part Two, Chapter 3. But just as one robin does not make a spring, one year's results do not make a case for active management. Successful investing is a long-term, disciplined, continuous process. We all know—or certainly should know—that long-term investors need to maintain calm and ignore short-term price changes—the zone within which that clever deceiver Mr. Market operates most effectively. Consider 2015. In the United States, the S&P 500 was up a mere 1 percent, while one cluster of nine stocks was up some 60 percent at year-end: the Nifty Nine[2]—Amazon, Facebook, Google, eBay, Microsoft, Netflix, Priceline, Salesforce, and Starbucks—had an average price-earnings ratio of 45, double the market average. So any active manager owning several of these nine stocks would look brilliant for 2015. But was it really luck or skill—and was it repeatable? Meanwhile, in the United Kingdom, energy stocks were down so much that any active manager who was light in the energy sector—and ideally heavy on small-capitalization stocks—won a major victory. But was it luck or skill? Only ample time—lots of time—can tell for sure, but history tells us how to bet.

9. *"Indexing did so well last year that active investing is sure to do better soon."* Maybe. But serious investing is not a one-year or two-year proposition. Over the long term, the record shows low-cost indexing does better than active management.

As you read this short book, please remember that I certainly have nothing against active investors. I was one myself—30 and 40 and 50 years ago. As a group, today's active investors are among the smartest, best-educated, hardest-working, most creative, disciplined, and interesting people in the world—surely the most capable collection of determined competitors the world has ever seen. So if you want to know whether you can retain the services of an excellent team of stellar people, fear not. You can, and with a little effort, you will. (Unless you reach for the impossible and catch a Bernie Madoff!)

You would not, however, be asking the right question. Every other investor will have the same objective and many will be equally able to select excellent managers.

The right question is this: Will your chosen manager be enough better than the other excellent managers over the long term—after costs, fees, and taxes—to regularly beat the collective expertise of all the many other investment experts? Alas, the realistic answer to *this* question is almost certainly no.

Here's why. To beat the market by a worthwhile margin, a manager would have to outperform the best work of over half a million smart, experienced, creative, disciplined, and highly motivated experts—all trying to beat each other after costs and fees. All these experts have superb educations and years of experience working with the best practitioners on a level playing field with the same wonderful technology, the same exposure to new concepts, the same immediate access to all sorts of superb information, and the same interpretations and advice from the same experts.

How substantial must that outperformance be? Let's look at the numbers: To outperform the stock market—now generally expected to average 7 percent annual returns—by just 1 percentage point requires a superiority in returns of over 14 percent ($1 \div 7 = 14.3$). If the manager charges a 1 percent fee, the necessary outperformance zooms to nearly 29 percent ($2 \div 7 = 28.6$). Even if fees are "only" half of 1 percent and beating the market by half of 1 percent is the objective (after fees, costs, and risk), the manager would still have to be 15 percent better than the other experts—year after year.

And *that* is the real challenge. Doing this *was* feasible 30 or 50 years ago, but not today.

Investment skill as opposed to luck is exceedingly hard to measure. Furthermore, measurement takes a long time because investing problems differ month to month and year to year and in many different ways, market environments differ, and the competition from other investors differs. Meanwhile, investment managers age, change roles, and accumulate assets to manage—among many other possible changes. By the time a masterful manager can be identified with certainty, chances are she or he has changed, too.

In a typical 12-month period, about 40 percent of mutual funds will beat the market. Even after taxes, 30 percent or more will succeed. (See Part Two, Chapter 2.) But can they succeed again and again over 10 years or 20 years or longer? Historical data say, "No, not likely." Over a decade, the "success" rate drops from 40 percent to 30 percent. And over 20 years, it drops again to just 20 percent; the other 80 percent fail to keep up.

As an investor, you will be investing for a very long time. Changing managers is so notoriously fraught with costs and risks that, if you could, you would want to stay with one superior manager. But the lesson of history is that superior active managers seldom *stay* superior for long, and changing managers is both costly and difficult.

So here comes the real difficulty: will you be able to select the manager *today* that will be superior in the future? Will that same manager still be superior in 20 years—or even 10 years? If your chosen manager fades or stumbles, as most once superior managers have, will you be able to recognize the looming decline in time to act? And will you then be able to select another exceptional manager for the next 10 or more years? The data on investors' experience are truly grim. Money flowing into and out of mutual funds shows that most investors all too often work against their own best interests when trying to pick managers. (Institutions do, too. On average, the managers they fire outperform the new managers they hire.) Starting from the date they earn their coveted ratings, top-rated funds typically underperform their chosen benchmarks.

To see the reality through an analogy, imagine yourself at an antique fair with dozens of open booths. When you arrive, hoping to find some lovely things for your home, you are told one of four stories.

In one story, you are the first to arrive and will have two hours—alone—to look over the merchandise and make your selections.

In the second story, you will be joined by two dozen other "special guest" expert shoppers for the same two hours.

In the third scenario, you will be admitted to do your shopping for two days along with 1,000 other special ticket holders, but not until shortly after the two dozen experienced "special guests" have spent two hours making their selections.

In the final scenario, you are one of 50,000 shoppers admitted, but only on the third day of the fair. In this last scenario, you may find a few objects you like at prices you believe are reasonable, but we both know you won't discover any antiques that are seriously mispriced bargains. Now make a few more changes: all the shoppers are not only buyers, they are also sellers, each bringing and hoping to sell antiques they recently purchased at other fairs—and all are looking for ways to upgrade their collections. In addition, the prices of all transactions—and all past transactions—are known to all market participants, and they all have studied antiques at the same famous schools and have ready access to the same curators' reports from well-regarded museums.

This simple exercise reminds us that open markets with many expert and well-informed participants will work well at their primary function: price discovery. The problem is certainly not that active investment managers are unskillful, but rather that they have been becoming more and more skillful for many years and in greater numbers. So, in its ironic way, this book is a celebration of the extraordinary past success of the world's active managers. While a purist can correctly claim that the major stock markets of the world aren't perfect at matching price to value at every moment, most prices are too close to value for any investor to profit from the errors of others by enough to cover the fees and costs of making the effort. In other words, while the market is not *perfectly* efficient, it's no longer worth the real costs of trying to beat the market.

If you can't beat 'em, you can join 'em by indexing, particularly for the Big Four reasons: (1) the stock markets have changed extraordinarily over the past 50 years; (2) indexing outperforms active investing; (3) index funds are low cost; and (4) indexing investment *operations* enables you as an investor to focus on the *policy* decisions that are so important for each investor's long-term investment success.

NOTES

1. "Removing the punch bowl …" is how William McChesney Martin described his role as chairman of the Board of Governors of the Federal Reserve (1951–1970).
2. John Authers reported on the Nifty Nine and their origin at Ned Davis Research in the *Financial Times,* November 29, 2015.

ACKNOWLEDGMENTS

Among the many joys of a long career in and around investment management are the privileges of friendships with bright, thoughtful, informed people of different ages, nationalities, and experiences who are actively engaged in the world's longest-running, widest-ranging, most exciting competitive contest—with each other, with the crowd, and always with oneself—this side of politics or world war.

Fate and circumstances have conspired with merry laughter to give me many remarkable chances to see and learn within the worldwide explosion of learning about investing over the past half-century: over 200 one- and two-week trips to London during more than three decades of transformation launched by Big Bang; another 50 weeks in Tokyo; and many thousands of meetings in New York City, Boston, Chicago, and other North American cities.

Friendships have been central to the learning experiences that have enabled me to recognize and reflect at length on the great 50-year bell curve of transformation of investment management that once made active or "performance" investing the glorious new new thing it once was and then drove it steadily into decline and demise.

Friends have, as so often before, rallied to help clarify, strengthen, and bring this book to fruition. Linda Koch Lorimer, my wife and best friend, read the first rough draft, celebrated its strengths, and correctly insisted on major changes. Then, a wide circle of friends critiqued the contents. Jim Vertin examined every page and was joined by Carla Knobloch, Jonathan Clements, David Rintels, Bill Falloon, John McStay, Heidi Fiske, Lea Hansen, Sarah Williamson, and Suzanne Duncan.

Brooke Rosati typed the many redrafts and revisions, humming with cheerful good humor and great patience.

Elizabeth McBride's deft editing and organizing suggestions were invaluable.

William Rukeyser, as he did with *The Partnership*—the story of Goldman Sachs's rise to leadership—reworked the whole on four different levels: overall structure, perspective, flow, and specific words. If the essential factor in a good friend is that he or she enables you to be better, then Bill is my very good friend—and the secret friend of every reader.

PART ONE

OVER 50 YEARS
OF LEARNING
TO INDEX

1

MY HALF-CENTURY ODYSSEY

Well into my second year at Harvard Business School (HBS), spring was coming, Boston's snow was melting, and classmates were accepting job offers when one of them asked one day at lunch, "Charley, have you decided on a job yet?"

"Not yet. Several good interviews, but no definite offers. Why do you ask?"

"My father has a friend who's looking for an MBA to work at Rockefeller. Could that interest you?"

Thinking he meant the Rockefeller Foundation, I said I was interested. "Great!" he said, "Expect a call from a man with an unusual name: Strange."

So I soon agreed to meet Robert Strange—at his suggestion in the remarkably unremarkable third-floor "apartment" of three rooms off one open landing in an old Victorian frame house where my wife and I were living. At the appointed time, Bob Strange rang the doorbell and cheerfully followed me up the stairs. Sitting together on secondhand chairs that might have come from Goodwill, we began to talk. After half an hour, I knew I could learn a lot from a man as thoughtful, informed, and articulate as Bob Strange, so if he offered me a job I would take it. But while it was becoming clear that he did *not* work at the Rockefeller Foundation, it wasn't clear what kind of work he did do. I'd better find out.

During the next half hour, I learned his work involved investing, a field I knew nothing about but that sounded interesting, and his employer was Rockefeller Brothers, Inc., which managed investments for Rockefeller family members and philanthropies they had endowed. The interview seemed to go well, and near the end Bob said, "Well, we've covered quite a lot of ground, Charley. Would you like to join us?" I said yes. Then Bob asked, "When would you like to start?" and, smiling, went on to suggest, "With vacations and all, summers are rather quiet, so why don't you come in on Tuesday after Labor Day?" I said "Fine. I'll be there," and that was that.

After Bob left, I went to tell my wife, who had been discreetly reading in the bedroom with the door closed. "Good news! I got the job."

"Great! What will you be doing?"

"Investing."

"Sounds interesting! What will you get paid?"

"Gosh, I forgot to ask."

Setting my pay at $6,000 was, I later learned, easy. That's what the Rockefeller bank—Chase Manhattan—paid first-year MBAs and also what the Family paid beginning domestic servants.

That was in 1963. Few of my Harvard Business School classmates went into investments and only a very few went to Wall Street. Several went into commercial banking, almost always for the training programs and a few years of experience before moving on to a corporate job—but almost never for a career.

• • •

"Chahley, Chahley, didn't you learn *anything* about investing at Hahvud?" My supervisor, Phil Bauer, had just finished reading my first report—on textile stocks—at Rockefeller Brothers, Inc. He was *not* pleased. My report was all too obviously the work of a rank beginner.

Confessing the obvious, I explained that the only course on investing at Harvard Business School was notoriously dull, given by a boring professor and dealing largely with the tedious routines of a local bank's junior trust officer administering trusts for the family of a wealthy widow, Miss Hilda Heald. Instead of the usual class size of 80, the course had only a dozen students—all looking for a "gut" course where decent grades were assured because the professor needed students for his course. Meeting from 11:30 to 1:00, the course was aptly known as Darkness at Noon.

"Well, Chahley, the Rockafellahs ah rich people, but not so rich they can afford a complete beginnah like *you!* You gotta learn somethin' about investin'—and *soon*!" Before the day was over, arrangements were made for me to join the training program at a Wall Street firm, Wertheim & Company, to learn the basics of securities analysis; to join the New York Society of Security Analysts so I could hear companies' presentations and meet other analysts; and to enroll in night courses on investment basics at New York University's downtown business school. Tuition would be paid so long as my grades were B+ or better—generous terms and important for a married guy living in New York City on a salary of $6,000. The fall term was about to begin, so I went to register for courses.

Arriving at a large room where a sign said REGISTRATION, I joined one of several long lines of twenty-somethings and eventually stood in front of a card table with a typewriter on it and a young woman sitting behind it. "Special or regular?" she asked. Since I didn't answer quickly, she rephrased her question: "Are you a special student or a regular student?"

"Can you explain the difference?"

"Sure, special students are just taking one or two courses; regular students are in a degree program. What's your latest school and last degree?"

"Harvard Business School—MBA."

"Oh wow! Harvard Business School! That's really great! Well, since you already have your MBA, you should be in our PhD program!"

"Does it cost more?"

"Same price. Why not try it? You can always drop out."

Since nobody in my family had ever earned a PhD, I thought, "Why not?" It might be interesting and it would surprise my sister and brother, who had always gotten higher grades. I signed up with no idea that it would take me 14 long years to complete the PhD.

At NYU, I took two courses three nights a week, starting with proudly traditional courses in securities analysis, where the older faculty showed us how to analyze financial statements, estimate capital expenditures and their incremental rates of return, and create flow-of-funds statements. We also learned, during the 15-minute break between classes, how to dash two blocks to the hamburger shop, wolf bites of hot hamburger with gulps of cold milkshake to obtain a tolerable average temperature, and dash back to class.

The theoretical part of my training came from courses taught by the younger faculty, who were excited about and deeply engaged in the then new world of efficient markets, Modern Portfolio Theory, and the slew of research studies made possible by large new databases.

The *practical* part of my training took far less time: six eye-opening months at Wertheim & Company. Training was led by Joseph R. Lasser, a superb financial analyst with a warm personality who enjoyed showing us that the accounts in financial reports were a language that could be translated into a superior understanding of business realities *if* you got behind the reported numbers. A patient teacher-coach—"Let me show you how … and then you show me you can do it"—Joe believed in clearly written reports because clear writing required clear thinking and thorough understanding of a company's business. Joe also believed each report should tell an investment story that would hold the reader's interest without ever promoting the stock beyond the two underlined words in the upper left corner of page one of each report: Purchase Recommendation.

As research director of a major securities firm and an accomplished financial analyst and investor, Joe was one of the first to become a Chartered Financial Analyst, or CFA. That new certification—presumptuously described as the equivalent of a Certified Public Accountant (CPA) or a Chartered Life Underwriter (CLU), which at first it certainly was not—would soon require passing three all-day written examinations that assessed the candidate's skills in financial analysis and portfolio management. Joe said he thought we should all enroll in the study program, take the exams, and earn CFA Charters.[1] So we sent off for the study materials and the list of books we should read, studied on our own, and took the exams—invariably given each year on the most beautiful Saturday in June.

I was declared too young to take the third and final exam in 1968, and had to wait a year to mature. That same year, that third exam devoted the entire afternoon to one essay question: "Please Comment" on a recently published article brazenly titled "To Get Performance, You Have to Be Organized for It." It advocated separating the operational roles of active portfolio managers from the policy-setting role of an investment committee. Frustrated to be told, "You're too young," I quietly savored a delicious irony: I had written that article for the January 1968 issue of *Institutional Investor* magazine.

The article championed pursuing higher rates of return by putting an individual, research-centered, swiftly acting portfolio manager in charge of managing a mutual fund or pension fund. While establishment banks and insurance companies were usually opposed to such unstructured investing because it seemed dangerously distant from fiduciary responsibilities, the high-performance results being achieved seemed compelling.

• • •

Fifty years ago, it seemed to me and to almost everyone else employed in investments entirely reasonable to believe that bright, diligent analysts and portfolio managers who were serious about doing their homework—interviewing senior corporate executives after several weeks of preparation, doing extensive financial analysis, studying industry trends and competing companies, interviewing customers and suppliers, and studying in-depth reports by Wall Street's leading analysts—could regularly do three things: buy stocks that were underpriced, given their prospects; sell stocks that were overpriced; and construct portfolios that would produce results clearly superior to the overall market. Those of us privileged to be participants in the new ways of managing investments knew we were part of a major change. So, of course, we were all confidently "active investors."

The dark decades of the 1930s, 1940s, and 1950s were giving way to an exciting era during the later 1960s. Just a few years before, Donaldson, Lufkin & Jenrette and several other new brokerage firms—Baker Weeks, Mitchell Hutchins, Faulkner Dawkins & Sullivan, Auerbach Pollack & Richardson—had been formed to provide in-depth research reports to the fast-growing mutual funds that were rapidly taking market share from the banks that managed the mushrooming assets of corporate and public pension funds.

Active investment managers were competing against two kinds of easy-to-beat competitors. Ninety percent of trading on the New York Stock Exchange was done by individual investors.[2] Some were day traders speculating on price changes and rumors. The others were mostly doctors, lawyers, or businessmen who bought or sold stocks once every year or two when they had saved several thousand dollars or needed cash to buy a house or make a tuition payment. They were, perhaps, advised by a retail stockbroker who may or may not have read a two-page, backward-looking, nonanalytical "tear sheet" from Standard & Poor's. Even with fixed commissions averaging 40 cents a share, the broker's earning a good living depended on high turnover in his customers' accounts. So his focus was on transactions by his customers. This made it exceedingly unlikely that the broker had time for research or serious thinking about investment strategy or portfolio structure.

Over the years, researchers found that individual investors—not you, not me, but that fellow behind the tree—*lost*, through their own efforts to "do better," some 30 percent of the returns of the mutual funds or the stocks they invested in.[3] For ambitious MBAs armed with in-depth research and easy access to virtually any corporate executive, and focusing entirely on the stock market, these innocent retail investors were not hard to beat: They were easy prey. Their status echoed a famous military observation by Heraclitus: "Out of every 100 men, 20 are real soldiers … the other 80 are just targets."

In private rooms at elite clubs and fancy restaurants, corporate executives in candid off-the-record talks outlined their strategic plans, their earnings expectations, their acquisition policies, their financing plans—and then answered probing questions by analysts and portfolio managers roughly the age of their grown children. Analysts following a company closely might meet executives at headquarters four to six times a year, conducting one-on-one interviews of an hour or more with 5, 10, or even more executives who told what they knew. These interviews were combined with information from important customers and suppliers and many pages of detailed financial analysis. A major research report might run over 50 pages—even 100 pages. One firm bound its reports in hard covers to signal their importance.

During the late 1960s, the great growth stocks like IBM, Xerox, Avon, and Procter & Gamble (P&G) skyrocketed, and so did a new group of conglomerates such as Litton Industries, Gulf & Western, and LTV. They created fast-rising reported earnings through debt leverage, acquisitions of companies with low price-earnings ratios, and accounting prestidigitation. Investment counsel firms concentrated investments in both kinds of dynamic stocks and reported much higher returns than their establishment competitors. Back then, conservative bank trust departments and insurance companies were structured to be deliberate and prudent. Senior executives, with most of their careers behind them, met weekly or monthly to compose "approved lists" of the blue-chip stocks that their subordinates could then buy. In stocks, unseasoned issues were avoided, dividends were prized, and buy and hold was standard to avoid taxes. In bonds, laddered maturities and holding to maturity were hallowed norms.

A dramatic change came into institutional investment management when A. G. Becker & Company introduced its Funds Evaluation Service. It collected, analyzed, and reported how each pension fund—and each manager of each pension fund—had performed, quarter by quarter, in direct comparison with other funds. This changed everything. When the reports came out, they would prove that the big banks and the insurance companies were underperforming the market—again and again—while the active managers were repeatedly outperforming.

A remarkable new desktop device[4] could provide an investor who typed in the New York Stock Exchange (NYSE) symbol of a stock with the most recent price, the day's high and low, and the trading volume. Previously, an investor had to call a broker or, or if he had one, watch the ticker tape that Thomas Edison had invented back in 1869. Like all the others, I worked with a slide rule (mine was a beautiful log-log-decatrix). We filled out spreadsheets on bookkeeping paper with No. 2 pencils and rummaged through the NYSE files of Securities and Exchange Commission (SEC) reports, hoping to find nuggets of information. We talked by phone with analysts covering companies we thought might be interesting. Bonds were—and should be—boring. Very few investors ever owned foreign stocks.

The work was interesting, but nobody expected to make much money—unless you uncovered a great growth stock, which was what we all secretly hoped to do. MBAs were uncommon. PhDs were never seen. Commissions still averaged 40 cents a share. All trading was paper based. Messengers with huge black boxes on wheels, filled with stock and bond certificates, scurried from broker to broker trying to complete "good deliveries" of stock and bond certificates. They are all gone now; automation displaced them years ago. Many other changes since then have been substantial, so a few reminders of what Wall Street was like 50 years ago will provide perspective:

- Brokers' research departments—then usually fewer than 10 people—were expected to search out "small-cap" stocks for the firm's partners' personal accounts. One major firm put out a weekly four-page report covering several stocks, but most of the time provided no research for customers. But new firms were starting to break all the rules, concentrating on and being well received for providing in-depth research to win burgeoning institutional business.

- Block trading—with firms acting as dealers rather than brokers—had traditionally been scorned as too risky by the partners of establishment firms, but was now starting to develop, if only in trades of up 5,000 shares. (Today, trades of 100,000 shares are routine, and 500,000-share trades are not uncommon.)

- Computers were confined to the back office or "cage." Computers were certainly not used in research or on trading desks.

In 1966, Charlie Williams, my HBS classmate, called and suggested I visit his employer, the research-based institutional stockbrokerage firm Donaldson, Lufkin & Jenrette (DLJ). After half a day of interviews, I was astonished by the offered salary—more than twice my current pay plus opportunity for a bonus, 15 percent profit sharing, and eventual stock ownership. Even better, I would be working with the leading investment managers at many of the nation's leading institutions in New York and Boston, the two centers of institutional investing.

DLJ and several other new "institutional" brokerage firms were different from traditional Wall Street firms. We worked harder for longer hours than people at those firms, thought we were smarter, knew we had more education, and were sure we knew much more about the investment prospects of the companies we studied and recommended to our clients. Portfolio managers at mutual funds and pension managers, the fast-growing institutions we focused on, were quicker to take action than the committee-centered, tradition-bound insurance companies and bank trust departments that still dominated institutional investing.

Our extraordinary self-confidence was reinforced by the media. Circulation at the *Wall Street Journal* was soaring, and major newspapers around the country were expanding their coverage of business and the stock market. Magazines like *Institutional Investor*, *Barron's*, and *Financial Analysts Journal* were widely read, and a book called *The Money Game*[5] was a national best seller. It explained what performance investing was all about and why anyone who could certainly should get on the bandwagon with one of the hot-shot active investment firms.

• • •

My first *Institutional Investor* article vigorously advocated an approach to investment management that was considered best practice by its young practitioners then, but would, in three decades, be as out of date as the Underwood typewriter. During that passage of time, the stock market had become dominated by hundreds of thousands of professional investors, who all have superb information technology (IT) equipment and the same instant access to copious information, and compete with each other to find any pricing errors made by others.

The article declared that a major, game-changing breakthrough was revolutionizing institutional investing. Any organization that hoped to be competitive in the coming decades would need to change from the obsolete policy-based "closed" organizational structure dominated by investment committees of near-retirement seniors to an "open" structure with decision making dominated by research-trained young portfolio managers who scrambled every day to beat the market *and* the competition.

The single objective of these new organizations was to maximize investors' returns. The successful new investment managers achieved superior operating results because they were better organized for performance than more traditional investors. Capital productivity (*not* capital preservation) dominated the structure and activities of their entire organizations, and the efforts of every individual were aimed at maximizing portfolio profit.

The new organizations, seeing the market differently than the traditionalists, redefined portfolio management and organized themselves to exploit a changing set of problems and opportunities. The article cited these untraditional examples of the apparent virtues of active trading:

- A short-term orientation is wrong only if the long-term view is more profitable. Holding a stock for a long time does not really avoid the risk of adverse daily, weekly, or monthly price changes, but does prevent taking profitable advantage of these changes.

- Only skilled risk takers can hope to achieve outstanding results, since high returns usually involve braving risk and uncertainty. Liquidity allows the portfolio manager to abandon a holding whenever the risk-opportunity ratio becomes unsatisfactory and therefore allows him to buy a stock that has high risks but even higher profit potential.

- Since large investors act on or in anticipation of current corporate developments, and market prices respond quickly to the new consensus, the profit-maximizing investment manager will move quickly to avoid price declines or to capture price increases.

- The stock market is a uniquely competitive arena in which the investment manager not only buys from but also sells to his competitors and, in general, can only buy from and can only sell to these competitors. To obtain superior results, he simply must be an outstanding competitor.

The new managers were convinced that the traditional organizational structure had important weaknesses that could be reduced or eliminated by changes in management organization and method. The competent individual would have important advantages over a committee in making decisions. In portfolio management, time is money, and the necessarily slow decision process of an investment committee looked very expensive in opportunity costs. Memoranda prepared for investment committees took analysts' time away from productive research efforts. Formal procedures delayed actions, often until, because of price changes, it was too late to act.

"The flow of money to these new managers is impressive evidence that the public recognizes their success. Investment managers that are organized along more traditional lines should seriously consider the nature and importance of the new approach to investment management." So I wrote and believed back in 1968. Only two years later, though, I began to see a few clouds on the performance horizon.

In my work at DLJ, I was in almost continuous contact with the portfolio managers and analysts at the major institutional investors in Boston, Hartford, New York City, and Philadelphia. This privileged experience showed me that while each institution knew it had bright, experienced, and highly competitive professionals, so did every other institution. "Performance investing is not nearly as easy as it looks to one of the noncombatants," I cautioned in a new article:

> Not only is performance investing hard to do, the most effective practitioners face serious problems that raise the question: Will success spoil performance investing? The problem with success is simple: You get too big, almost "money bound" and increasingly limited to "big-cap" stocks and paying high tolls in transition costs to get in or out of each position, the costs of operation increase, and there is not enough profit from good ideas to go around. That's why success is beginning to spoil performance investing.[6]

• • •

"You can observe a lot," proclaimed America's folk hero Yogi Berra, "just by watching." As usual, he was right—as

22

I would find out when studying the academic literature in preparation for my PhD oral examination a few years later. While there were continuing arguments over specific questions among academics, the major concepts of market efficiency had been fully resolved. Practitioners who ignored the evidence would continue to scoff, but the more data gathered and analyzed, the easier it was to make a convincing, fact-based case that stock markets, while not perfectly efficient, were becoming too efficient for most active managers to beat, particularly after fees. But that reality failed to discourage those devoting their time, skills, and energy to beating the market and earning a handsome living through active, "performance" investing.

Back in the late 1960s and early 1970s, the differences in the prevailing academic view of active investing versus the prevailing view of leading practitioners were substantial—and have been remarkably enduring ever since. In one way, I was caught in a crossfire, but in another way, I had the best of both worlds. My PhD degree depended on mastering the academic, but my day job depended on mastering the pragmatic. There were, it became clear, two cultures on Wall Street. One, clearly taking control at university finance faculties, held traditional practitioners in disdain—evenly matched by the disdain in which practitioners held the academics. The two camps believed in totally different concepts, used different data and different methods to support their different beliefs, spoke and wrote in different jargons, communicated with different constituencies, and continuously talked past each other. Few corporate executives read the academic journals reporting the theory and supporting evidence on indexing and the increasing evidence-based doubts about active investing. Academics, writing for their academic colleagues and using formal equations with Greek letters and arcane terms, didn't care. Corporate executives were not part of their intellectual community. If anything, acclaim within the ivory tower made it even less likely that pragmatic corporate executives would want to listen to new ideas expressed in unfamiliar language that seemed in conflict with their confident beliefs.

The academic world believed the evidence was both consistent and overwhelming and that there was no reason to keep arguing.

Academics agreed that the securities markets are open, free, competitive arenas where large numbers of informed and price-sensitive professionals compete as both buyers and sellers in price discovery, so markets are efficient at processing information to discover the correct price of each security. Around this correct price, specific prices will deviate in a "random walk." Investment managers operating in this stock market will not be able to find patterns in these market prices that will enable them to predict future price changes on which they can profit.[7] Moreover, because other competing investors are also well-informed buyers and sellers—particularly in the aggregate—it's unlikely that any one investment manager can regularly obtain profit increments for a large portfolio through fundamental research.[8]

The assertion that a market is efficient implies that current prices reflect all that is knowable about the companies whose stocks are being traded.[9] While there is some specialized evidence that quarterly earnings reports[10] and information on insider transactions[11] are not immediately and completely discounted in securities prices, the opportunities to be exploited are very limited, so managers of large funds will not be able to make effective use of this kind of information. The conclusion was clear: markets were too efficient for active managers to do better.

Academics consequently believe that financial analysis and security analysis are unprofitable activities. Evidence derived from observing a large number of professionally managed portfolios over a long time shows that not only were these funds not able, on average, to predict securities prices well enough to outperform a simple buy-the-market-and-hold investment policy, but also that there was little evidence that any *individual* fund would be able to do significantly better than would be expected from mere random chance.[12] The chances are that the securities the investment manager sells after doing fundamental research, and the stocks he doesn't buy will do about as well as the stocks he does buy. Some of the information he gets will be valid, but some will be invalid, and he won't know which is which. What he gains on good information, he will lose on bad information, so, taken as a whole, the information he gets will not be valuable.[13] Not only did academics declare investment managers unable to predict prices for individual securities successfully, they found managers unable to predict price movements for the market as a whole.

Academics believed that, as a result of their inability to make superior predictions of security prices, either individually or in aggregate, investment managers were unlikely to outperform a passive buy-the-market-and-hold portfolio strategy. Their evidence supported the theoretical expectation: professionally managed portfolios had, on average, done no better than the market.[14]

Practitioners had not begun to fight, nor did they feel any need to. Active management was obviously better. They knew they were smart, creative, and hardworking. They saw opportunities every day. Oh, sure, there might be rough patches here and there, but they knew they would win in the long run. After all, they were the best and brightest.

I grappled with exactly these matters in my PhD dissertation. Table 1.1 summarizes the two views.

The difference between the academic and practitioner views back in the 1970s could easily be explained by observing both in an historical context. In the first place, the academic view was relatively new—less than 10 years old. In practical terms, index funds had been in operation only since 1971, when Wells Fargo began managing a fund for the pension plan of Samsonite Corporation. No index fund was available to individual investors. The practitioners' view was internally consistent, which gave it strength in resisting major changes in either concept or technique. Moreover, the notion of achieving superior results by devoting outstanding professional resources to the task of investment management was intuitively appealing.

Table 1.1 Summary of Academic View and Practitioner View

Topic	Academic View	Practitioner View
Ability of investment managers to outperform the market averages	No evidence to support this belief; probability of success at best very low; not possible to identify in advance which managers will do so.	Can be done by many managers. Past results and capabilities of an investment organization can be used as evidence to select managers that can be expected to succeed in the future.
Fees to managers	A cost that should be minimized by explicit policy because higher fees obtain little or no benefit for the investor.	A cost that should be accepted gladly to obtain the services of superior managers that will outperform the market by more than enough to warrant the fee.
Index funds	Should be used widely because their long-term results will be superior in both predictability and rate of return versus active management.	Should not be used because superior active managers can be identified, and clients should seek out those superior managers.

Most of the academic research had been reported primarily in journals not usually read by investors. Research findings were generally presented in mathematical formulations that were unfamiliar and might even be intimidating. Few books dealt effectively with the subject on a nontechnical level, and the seriously selective information clients had been getting through conventional communication channels continued to support the traditional view of investment management.

• • •

Hindsight makes clear that active investing was going through the early stages of an elongated, half-century version of the classic bell-curve life cycle of innovation: small, hard-won gains; then larger and larger gains made more easily and more rapidly; then, at a somewhat slower pace, still more gains; then, even more slowly, smaller and smaller gains; then, after peaking, small declines that would grow larger and larger.

By 1971, while I was still fairly optimistic about the opportunities available to active investment managers, the increasing difficulty of achieving significantly superior performance was becoming evident. The number of active investment firms had increased substantially, and not all had been successful. In another article in the *Financial Analysts Journal*, I observed:

> *Game theorists describe as zero sum those situations in which neither side will gain a significant advantage unless the other side suffers an equally significant failure. And if, over the long haul, the players are as evenly matched in skills, information, experience, and resources as professional investors today certainly appear to be, little systematic advantage will be gained and maintained by any of the players and their average annual experience will be to lag behind the market by the cost to play.*[15]

When selling their capabilities, investment managers still exuded confidence in their ability to prevail in the highly competitive money game. All those who got to selection finals had the gee-whiz charts of superior past results and the compelling projections of surefire winners, and they dressed their parts. Investors were sure they could and would find talented, deeply committed managers with impressive records who would beat the market for them. Institutional investors, often with the help of well-known consultants, in a bake-off with three to five finalists would choose the best. No matter that the rates of return were not risk adjusted. No matter that the record's starting date might be carefully chosen to make the manager look good. No matter that the benchmark with which comparisons were made might be selected from a variety of possibilities. Investment managers soon learned that the dominant factor in most institutions' manager selection decisions was "performance," particularly over the past few years. Little did it matter that past performance has been shown to have almost no power to predict future investment performance. In the scramble to find "top-quartile" managers, there would be no interest in settling for averages or in *passive* investing. No matter that the manager might select certain of its funds that showed the best results. And no matter that the selected data for the selected fund for the selected period were often reported "gross" of fees—*before* fees were deducted.

Active investment managers assured clients and prospects that they would beat the market by significant margins.[16] In their drive to win more business, which would produce wide incremental profit margins, investment managers engaged in modest deceptions to look their best in review meetings, sales meetings, brochures, and media advertisements. They would, wouldn't they? Believing numbers don't lie, few clients were familiar with the difficulties of evaluating long-term and complex continuous processes with small samples of only a few years of data—samples that often were seriously biased by retroactive deletions of failed funds or late and also retroactive additions of successful funds. (See Part Two, Chapter 2.)

• • •

Shortly after my classmates and I left Harvard Business School, mutual funds and pension funds were growing rapidly in assets and were increasing portfolio turnover in a quest for superior performance.[17] A dynamic young professor named Colyer Crum created an entirely different course that caught the leading edge of what would become a major revolution in institutional investing: the first-ever course on professional investing. It was a phenomenal success. Within two years, it was taught six times each year to nearly 500 students. Only 100 of the MBA students did *not* take the course. Professor Crum came to one of the early portfolio manager seminars I'd been leading for DLJ. At the seminar, Colyer insisted, with his usual provocative style, that those who did not accept the burgeoning new reality were doomed to experience disruptive innovations.

Colyer invited me to be a guest speaker in his new course and then, after that one class, invited me to teach an 80-student section of his course on institutional investing. Understandably, my wife did not react positively. "You are doing too much already, including studying for your PhD. You can't teach a whole Harvard Business School course, too!" She was right, of course, so I declined. But a year later, the "to die for" invitation was renewed. The demand for the course had surged, and I would have two sections of 80 students. Accepting the invitation, I decided, would require being away from home only one night each week. This could be done by flying to Boston as early as possible on the first day of classes each week.

This would work if I cut everything close: take the 7:00 A.M. Eastern Airlines shuttle out of LaGuardia to

Boston's Logan in time to catch a taxi to the school—arriving just in time for class at 8:40. Ollie's Taxi Service agreed to pick me up at home at 6:10 that first morning and take me to LaGuardia, but Ollie overslept and came badly late, still in his pajamas. He promised to drive as fast and aggressively as humanly possible; I promised a big tip if we made it on time. Because of heavy snow during the week before, traffic was slow, but Ollie took chances. By the time we got to Eastern's very temporary "terminal" at LaGuardia, it was already flight time. I ran 50 yards to the gate.

"Too late!" cried out the gate agent, as he saw me coming—and gestured to the Convair that was folding its stairway up and into itself. Seeing my intention, he barked: "You *cannot* go out there!" I pushed my ticket into his chest and ran out onto the tarmac. The pilot looked down at me from the cockpit. I gestured with both arms outstretched, palms up, in a silent plea for mercy.

Please. *Please.*

For the first and only time in my life, the plane's stairs were reextended. I scrambled aboard. Out of breath, I fell into a seat and buckled up, knowing that fate must be on my side—again. Unless something went terribly wrong, I was not going to be a disastrous hour late for my first class at HBS. At Logan, I ran to get the first taxi. More snow made traffic slow, but the driver knew a back route and, when I promised a $20 tip, drove as though *he* were late for class—including running two red lights. He earned the full $20, and I walked quickly toward my assigned classroom.

Working my way through the crowd of students, I was 10 feet from the door to Aldrich 108 and just two minutes before the 8:40 start of my first class when I recognized the man coming the other way: Paul Lawrence, one of my favorite teachers. Knowing I was there to teach my first class—just seven years after graduation—he smiled warmly and gently wished me the one thing I had already so much lots of that morning: "Good luck!"

• • •

The course went well, more than fulfilling my hopes. The last of the 34 sessions centered on a critical question: with all the analytical talent and computer power being gathered into the many new investment firms, was it possible that they would make markets so much more efficient or correctly priced that most investment firms would be unable to beat the market? Near the end of the last class, one of the students asked, "Charley, we all know the school does not allow the faculty to declare their own views because you want us to think for ourselves. But just this once, please tell us what *you* really think."

Silence—and 80 expectant faces waiting.

"I believe that it's clearly possible to organize a first-rate group of analysts and portfolio managers into an investment firm that can significantly outperform the market averages."

Pause.

"And … I'm wrong!"

Class dismissed.

• • •

At NYU, the younger faculty, committed to such new ideas as efficient markets and Modern Portfolio Theory, were in a Young Turks struggle with the Old Guard to take control of the PhD program. My academic adviser made it clear that the only way I could pass the comprehensive exam, which he had personally designed, was to become proficient in the new thinking. So, of course, that's what lay ahead: 18 months of reading articles and books about how and why serious academic researchers were convinced that, while there was still room for argument about the "strong form" versus the "semi-strong form" of market efficiency, extensive examination of the data then becoming available proved time and time again that markets were surprisingly efficient—and that analysts and portfolio managers, still using slide rules, were surprisingly *in*efficient in making decisions to buy or sell stocks.

Another call came from HBS five years after my prior faculty appointment. Colyer Crum's course had been taken over by Jay O. Light.[18] To avoid being away more than one night a week, I arranged to meet with Boston clients of Greenwich Associates, the consulting firm I had launched in 1972, on the same day that classes met. I could teach two classes of 80 students each morning and be downtown working with clients by noon. Sensing that the Institutional Investment course might have changed, I made inquiries and was startled by the magnitude of change and glad I'd learned efficient market theory at NYU. As Jay put it, "We now begin at about where you concluded five years ago. Everyone comes into the class already having learned during first-year finance about Modern Portfolio Theory."

The class culture had also changed. Five years before, knowing students would be disappointed to have a "visiting fireman" instead of Colyer Crum, I had decided to master most of the students' names from picture cards given to the faculty. I'd impressed the students by calling out "Mr. Smith" or "Mr. Jones" to those with hands raised to participate in class discussion. Hoping for another success, I decided to try the same stunt. The presence of numerous women in the class was not the only change, as I found out when one of them, Laura Daignault, came toward me at the end of class. "You can call me Laura. We're all on a first-name basis at HBS." Ouch! Back I went to my flash cards to learn 160 *first* names.

• • •

One of the early clients of Greenwich Associates was a unit of San Francisco's Wells Fargo Bank[19] led by James Vertin.[20] He had sponsored a small group of creative "quants" or quantitative analysts to develop the first capitalization-weighted index fund for Samsonite's pension fund. (Their earlier "index" fund was not really an index fund because, instead of being capitalization weighted with each stock held in proportion to its market capitalization, it had weighted all stocks equally, Jim was confident that his team had found a rational pathway to successful index investing. Consulting on business development year after year with Jim and his team, I became confident that low-cost indexing could be a winning investment strategy—even if it was a hard sale.

Always looking for ideas for the three-day DLJ seminars for investment practitioners, I scheduled one of the five working sessions as an exploration of the academics' research and the practical application of it via indexing. Time and again, however, discussing indexing and Modern Portfolio Theory met with zero interest. I was cautioned more than once to "be careful with all that academic stuff, Charley." Active managers did not need to learn about it: they instinctively knew indexing had to be bogus. When leading academics were invited to participate in the seminars, the investment professionals made little effort to explore the evidence or the logic behind their views. Nor did the usually gregarious investors make any effort to befriend the academics. It was odd to watch the two groups—like two separate tribes—keeping their distance when both groups had so much to learn from each other.

Establishing Greenwich Associates as the leading consultant in institutional financial services was demanding more and more of my time and energy. One evening, as snow began to fall, my six-year-old son Harold, who had a new shovel, and I went out to shovel a little snow in the light of the streetlamps. After a while, thinking he might like to rest, I suggested we stop and talk.

"How's school, Harold?"

"Good. I like my teacher." Then he asked me, "And how's school for you, Dad?"

"The new firm really takes so much time and effort, it looks like I'll have to stop, Harold."

"Have you finished?"

"No, I haven't finished."

"Well, you know, Dad, you can't stop school until you finish," and he turned to start shoveling snow again. The next day, I was back in school, determined to complete the PhD.

Meanwhile, in Greenwich Associates' research on investment managers, most of the investment firms that made it to the Top 10 or Top 20 managers could not stay up there very long. Working with investment consulting firms confirmed that, despite extraordinary efforts, pension executives were unable to select managers that would consistently beat the market.

• • •

The early history of index funds was short. Wells Fargo's first index fund for Samsonite Corporation invested approximately $8 million in a sample of 100 stocks to match the performance of the New York Stock Exchange index.[21] It was not a success. Shortly thereafter, Wells

Fargo created a second fund, open to any pension fund. Based on the Standard & Poor's 500 stock index, it was called The Index Fund. By 1974, Wells Fargo had been joined by two other indexing firms: Batterymarch Financial Management and American National Bank. But neither of these two organizations had any clients for the new service.[22]

The first index mutual fund open to individual investors—First Index Investors Trust—was started by two remarkably innovative entrepreneurs, John C. Bogle of Vanguard and Dean F. LeBaron of Batterymarch (both were friends of mine and clients of Greenwich Associates, as was Jim Vertin at Wells Fargo). LeBaron had developed the software for indexing and was pursuing the institutional market. Jack Bogle, a creative and driven entrepreneur—who would later be widely admired as Saint Jack, the brave and strong centurion-advocate of the regular, everyday investors—was also a skillful reader of legal documents. Bogle was determined to break out of the box in which most observers believed he was confined forever to "back office" shareholder services by the separation agreement he had signed when he left Wellington Management Company. The agreement restricted him to administrative roles. By a narrow margin, Bogle convinced the Vanguard board of directors to support a strategic move. It appeared to be trivial but would, after a painfully slow start, become a triumph. Asserting that a well-run index fund needed only formulaic "administration," *not* "investment management," Bogle got authorization to distribute an index fund and then contracted with LeBaron's Batterymarch to operate that first index mutual fund.

While Bogle was preparing to launch his index mutual fund for individuals, AT&T sponsored a series of seminars in 1974 and 1975 for Bell System companies, then the largest pension fund complex in the nation, to inform executives of the logical case for index funds and to encourage them to adopt index matching on an experimental basis. A year earlier, Illinois Bell, the first Bell System affiliate to adopt index funds, had assigned $10 million—only about 3 percent of its total pension fund—to index management by Wells Fargo.[23]

By the end of 1975, New Jersey Bell and Southern Bell had placed $20 million and $50 million, respectively, with Batterymarch; New York Telephone had placed $50 million with the American National Bank; and Western Electric had placed $50 million with Wells Fargo.[24] In all these cases, the amounts placed in index funds were small relative to the total pension funds—in Western Electric's case, 2 percent of total assets. John English of AT&T said he believed the Bell System would invest as much as one-third of its equity—or $2.3 billion—in index funds "in the foreseeable future."[25] Around the same time, other companies began to experiment with indexing, including Exxon and Ford.[26] Pension funds' index investments rose from $18 million in 1971 to $2.9 billion by midyear 1977.

In the fall of 1974, Nobel Laureate Paul Samuelson had written "Challenge to Judgment,"[27] an article arguing that a passive portfolio would outperform a majority of active managers and pleading for a fund that would replicate the Standard & Poor's (S&P) 500 index. Two years later, in his regular *Newsweek* column, Samuelson reported, "Sooner than I expected, my explicit prayer has been answered" by the launch of the Bogle-LeBaron First Index Fund.

Samuelson notwithstanding, the First Index launch was not a success. Planned to raise $150 million, the offering raised less than 8 percent of that, collecting only $11,320,000. As a "load" fund, with an 8.5 percent sales charge, aiming to achieve only average performance, it could not gain traction. The fund then had performance problems. While outperforming over two-thirds of actively managed funds in its first five years, in the next few years it fell behind more than three-quarters of equity mutual funds. High fixed brokerage commissions were one problem. A larger problem came with "tracking" difficulties. To minimize costs, the portfolio did not own all the smaller-capitalization stocks in the S&P 500. Instead, it sampled the smaller stocks just as that group enjoyed an unusually strong run, so the fund failed to deliver on its "match the market" promise.

Renamed Vanguard Index 500 in 1980 and tracking the index closely, the fund grew to $100 million in 1982, but only because $58 million—more than half—came by merging into the fund another Vanguard fund "that had outlived its usefulness." Finally, as index funds began to gain acceptance with some investors, the Vanguard fund reached $500 million in 1987.[28]

Indexing was beginning to make inroads in the investment establishment. In 1976, *Fortune* reported that Bankers Trust's pension-fund division "believed that index funds were particularly desirable for employee-thrift and profit-sharing plans. With an index fund, the company can tell employees that it is simply 'buying the market' and it would then be protected against hindsight charges that it failed to deliver as promised."

A prominent Wall Streeter who had reluctantly accepted the case for index funds was Gustave Levy, senior partner of Goldman Sachs. Levy, a leader in large-scale block trading, did not take readily to index funds, which, of course, meant less trading and fewer commissions for brokers. But as a member of the pension committee of New York Telephone's board of directors, he gave the critical nod of approval for the company's investment in American National's index fund.

"None of us were negative on it," Levy said. "You couldn't be. Personally, I don't like the concept of the index fund, but, unfortunately, I have no arguments against them. I feel we ought to do better than the averages, but over long periods of time, managers can't beat the averages."[29]

• • •

Meanwhile, my own thinking had continued to evolve and change as I kept learning: In addition to the lucky accident of consulting with each of the leading index fund managers, I was getting a pragmatic education in the power of indexing. The disappointing experiences of our other clients who were active investors continued to give strong evidence of how difficult it had become to beat the market. I was also working with Bob Brehm at

A. G. Becker in Chicago on building that firm's new Funds Evaluation Service to measure investment performance. This immersed me in the overwhelming evidence that a majority of active managers were falling short of their chosen benchmarks, just as the academics had been predicting. At the *Financial Analysts Journal*, I served as an associate editor with its editor and market theorist Jack Treynor. Jack understood efficient markets and indexing thoroughly and explained why he believed it was sure to succeed. I also got to know William Burns, who had trained as an engineer and was treasurer of AT&T, guiding the Bell System companies toward indexing (and who later became a director of Greenwich Associates).

Consulting on strategy with leading active investment managers all over America, I was exposed as a trusted adviser to many investment firms. Each firm thought it was unusual, and they *were*. But I noticed an important reality they could not see because they did not have the access I had to many other firms' people, capabilities, and commitment. Compared to the many other superstar investment firms they were competing with, they were *not* unusual in capabilities nor in commitment. Moreover, the SEC's Regulation FD (Fair Disclosure) would eventually require that all information that might be useful to *any* investor must be made available simultaneously to *all* investors, thus making exclusive information and insight—once the secret sauce of successful active investors—into mere "everybody knows" commodities.

Professor James Lorie of the University of Chicago urged a constructive view of indexing: "Some people say that if you accept market funds, you are accepting mediocrity. You're not; you're accepting superiority. Market funds have been superior year after year—five-year period after five-year period, decade after decade—for as long as these measurements have been made. The people who seek superiority by trying to play the timing and selection games correctly have—on the average and with no single conspicuous exception—had worse performance than a market fund."[30]

Conventional active investment management became subject to sporadic skepticism during the 1970s. As a trade magazine commented early in the decade, "Just a few years ago, everyone was expecting to do at least 25 percent better than the S&P 500 and many investment counselors, in their [sales] efforts to pry the pension business away from the banks, were promising 50 percent."[31] The same article, reporting data that showed rates of return in managed pension funds to be lower than the unmanaged S&P 500 index, said, "There is plenty of evidence that professional money managers, on balance, fail to turn in superior performance. A. G. Becker's study of the performance of the equity portion of 300 large pension funds for the 11 years ended December 31, 1972, shows that the median fund returned 7.8 percent per year. Over the same period, the S&P 500 was up 8.1 percent. Of course, the reality that the *average* fund underperformed the stock market only increased the determination among clients to try to discover and hire top-quartile managers who, they hoped, would consistently produce superior results.

Active managers typically asserted that somehow the evidence was inaccurate, misrepresented, or incomplete. The Investment Company Institute, the trade association of the mutual fund industry, ran an ad showing that $10,000 invested in the average mutual fund 23 years before would have grown to be $103,898 by the end of 1972, for an average annual return of 10.7 percent. Jack Bogle, then president of Wellington Management Company, the manager of a large balanced fund, pointed out that if the computation had been limited to the all-equity mutual funds, the ending value would have approximated a nicely higher $120,000, for an overall rate of return of 11.4 percent. The article's writer went on to report, "But in the 23 years ended December 31, 1972, the S&P 500—which most major index funds were designed to replicate—had risen by [a significantly higher] 13.2 percent per year."[32]

Harvard Business School Professor Jay O. Light observed: "The 1969–1970 bear market caused enormous disenchantment among investors with professional money managers. People no longer believe the professionals' inflated claims that they can beat the market averages by 20 percent to 30 percent, and it's only a matter of time before a lot of investors start questioning whether the pros can outperform the average at all."[33]

Institutional investors often responded with sophistry, claiming that their relative performance during the early 1970s had somehow been unusually adversely affected by the recent bear market and that they would outperform again when more normal upward trending markets returned. But then, in 1975, when the market rose by more than one-third, most institutional investors' portfolios failed to keep pace, let alone achieve superior performance. A major *New York Times* article said, "There is plenty of evidence that professional money managers, on balance, fail to turn in superior performance. This relatively poor performance undoubtedly will add fire to the argument of those who believe money managers should invest some part of their assets in so-called market index funds."[34] As Table 1.2 shows, not only did the performance of the median pension fund measured by A. G. Becker fall short of the S&P 500, but the magnitude of the shortfall got worse in each successive cycle.

Table 1.2 Performance of the Median Pension Fund

	S&P 500 Index	Becker Median	Difference
Three market cycles 9/30/62 to 12/31/74	5.3%	4.1%	−1.2%
Two market cycles 12/31/66 to 12/31/74	2.1%	0.4%	−1.7%
Single market cycle 9/30/70 to 12/31/74	2.2%	−0.3%	−1.9%

Analysis showed that the unmanaged S&P 500 index ranked consistently in the upper quartile among several hundred actively managed equity portfolios of pension funds in the Becker sample.[35] In addition to lagging the index, studies also found that 90 to 95 percent of professionally managed equity portfolios had been more *risky* than the S&P 500 as measured by relative volatility.[36] Paul Samuelson chimed in: "What is at issue is not whether, as a matter of logic or brute fact, there are managers capable of doing better than the average on a repeatable, sustainable basis. There is nothing in the mathematics of random walks or Brownian movements that proves or even postulates that it is impossible. The crucial point is that when investors look to identify those minority groups or methods that are endowed with sustainable superior investment prowess, they are quite unable to find them."[37]

In the summer of 1975, the *Financial Analysts Journal* published my article "The Loser's Game," crystallizing my conclusions about the low chances of active managers beating the market regularly because, due to the growth of institutional investing, they *were* the market and their skills and efforts were creating a major problem for all active managers: superb competition. While "The Loser's Game" won the Graham & Dodd award as the year's best article in the *Financial Analysts Journal*, most professional investors patronizingly said that they appreciated the concept and reasoning but went right ahead with their customary practices and with their same expectations to succeed—apparently confident that the article's thesis might apply to many *other* investors but not to them.

• • •

The early proponents of indexing, understandably enamored of the technology of their operations, concentrated on (and forced prospects to listen to) detailed technical explanations of how their index funds worked. Advocates of indexing might quantify their case with data, but those who felt uncomfortable with algebraic equations fought back: "Passive is giving up and is for losers!" "Nobody ever won by settling for just average!" Besides, opponents of indexing could always find at least a few active managers who had outperformed.

Nobody will ever know just how much harm was done by wrapping the term *passive* around indexing, but it certainly was not trivial. We do know that the most popular insurance product had little success until its name was changed from death insurance to life insurance. Indexers, trained as engineers and mathematicians, may never have realized how much names matter. But doing better by working harder and smarter and knowing more than the average has long been central to our competitive culture. Names do matter. To prove it, try saying, "This is my husband. He's … *passive*." Or "Our football team captain is … *passive*." Or "What America needs is a president who is … *passive*." Future growth of indexing will gain strength if and when *passive*—with all its negative implications—disappears from our thinking.

The process by which new or different concepts are accepted by those who can use them is seldom speedy or reliable or efficient. Charles Darwin believed that his theory of evolution would not achieve general acceptance until his professional generation had all died off. On the occasion of the paperback release of John Maynard Keynes's *The General Theory of Interest and Money* 29 years after the book's original publication in England, John Kenneth Galbraith explained in his review: "The economists of established reputation had not taken to Keynes. Faced with the choice of changing one's mind versus proving that there is no need to do so, almost everyone opts for the latter."[38] Two more decades would pass before an American president would publicly acknowledge that he was a Keynesian.

The way worldviews change is discussed by Thomas S. Kuhn in *The Structure of Scientific Revolutions*. While

Kuhn's concern was with changes in scientific theories, his analysis of the process of change is relevant to the acceptance of any fundamentally new concept—including index funds. Kuhn wrote:

> *Any new interpretation of nature, whether a discovery or a theory, emerges first in the mind of one or a few individuals. It is they who first learn to see the world differently, and their ability to make the transition is facilitated by two circumstances that are not common to most other members of their profession. Invariably their attention has been intensely concentrated upon the specific crisis-provoking problem. In addition, they usually are so young or so new to the crisis-ridden field that not having many years of past practice has committed them less deeply than most of their contemporaries to the world view and the rules of the old paradigm.*[39]

Resistance to indexing continued for a long time. But as the years went by, and the markets changed and competition increased, the logical and economic case for indexing grew stronger and stronger. As Figures 1.1 and 1.2

Figure 1.1 Index Mutual Funds

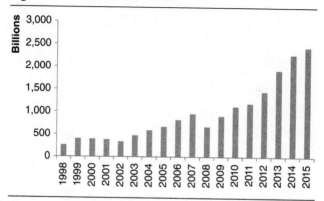

Source: 2016 Morningstar, Inc.

Figure 1.2 Index ETFs

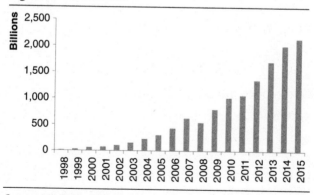

Source: 2016 Morningstar, Inc.

show, demand for index funds has been increasing at an accelerating rate.

• • •

The data that were persuasive to academics were not decisive or compelling to pension fund or mutual fund executives—the people who would have to make the change from active managers to index funds and would be accountable to their superiors if experience did not confirm their decisions. The vigorous, widespread blow-back by active managers carried the day. During the winter of 1977, a poster appeared in the offices of investment management companies nationwide depicting Uncle Sam stamping "Un-American" on computer printouts and the words: "Help Stamp Out Index Funds. Index Funds Are Un-American."[40]

Not surprisingly, much of the investment community took a dim view of both the random-walk theory—that market price changes are as unpredictably random as the steps made by a drunk unsure which way to go home—and index funds. The head of a major investment firm asserted, "It's a cop-out that you can't do better than the averages. I know from the numbers that most managers don't beat the averages, but I don't feel that is any reason for giving up."[41] More of this generalized data-free resistance was described in an article in the *Wall Street Journal:* "Not surprisingly, the concept of index funds infuriates the traditional investment community. 'I hope the damn things fail because if they don't, it's going to mean the jobs of a lot of good analysts and portfolio managers,' says an officer of a major Boston bank."

The basic idea of being "only average" antagonized many investment managers. When the New York City pension funds began investing in index funds in the mid-1970s, the *New York Times*, in an article entitled "Why Indexing Frightens Money Managers," quoted Dave H. Williams, then chairman of the investment committee of Mitchell Hutchins & Company: "It's an avenue for seeking mediocrity."[42]

The CEO of a prominent investment firm, David Babson, asked, "What's so great about matching the S&P? Index funds are a negative approach. The S&P itself represents two-thirds of the market value of all stocks and so, by definition, cannot provide above-average results. If you settle for simply matching it, you're throwing in the towel—you're conceding defeat."[43] Another way of arguing against index funds was to declare them to be just a fad and to associate them with other investment fads that had failed. Or, as another money manager put it, index funds are just another case of a response to something that has already happened, and, as such, represent an idea whose time has passed."[44]

Barton Biggs, the much admired Morgan Stanley partner in charge of investment research, wrote an extended essay for distribution to his firm's institutional investor clientele in which he attacked the thinking of two commentators who had written popular articles that argued in favor of indexing[45]:

> *Both ... make several important mistakes that undermine their entire thesis. ... The first error is they maintain that professional money managers cannot outperform the market. While it is true that professional money managers have not beaten the market in recent years, prior to 1970 they vastly outperformed the S&P.*[46]

Barton was right about the past, but not about the future. In 1976, the year at the start of which he wrote his essay, the total return on the S&P 500 was 24.0 percent, 4.7 percentage points greater than the return on the median actively managed equity fund.

In a letter to the *Wall Street Journal,* Erwin Zeuschner, director of research at Chase Manhattan Bank, stretched the early trend to future extremes and argued that *the proliferation of index funds would lead to massively* inefficient *markets and a stock's price would become more a function of monies flowing into index funds than a reflection of its investment merits. The entire capital allocation process of the securities markets would be distorted, and only companies represented in indexes would be able to raise equity capital.*[47]

Concern over the potentially adverse impact of index funds on the capital markets was expressed by others, including the investment company Scudder, Stevens & Clark: "If everyone following an index fund approach adhered to the S&P 500 as the surrogate for the market portfolio, it would likely lead to an overvaluation of those securities relative to the other securities in the market. The very premise of the index fund strategy would crumble."[48] But, in contrast to the theoretical alarm, when Standard & Poor's changed the S&P 500 by adding 45 stocks and simultaneously deleting 45 other stocks, Dean LeBaron of Batterymarch, then one of the largest index fund managers, said, "We were able to make all the changes within the week in which they were announced with no market impact."[49]

In January 1976, when the New York City pension funds, working through Goldman Sachs, sold a huge $240 million in stocks and bought $239 million in other stocks to create an index fund—all in one month—traders at other block trading firms were not able to detect the massive move even though it was widely known that such a large move was in the offing.[50] In fact, two weeks *after* the trades were completed, brokers were still calling—trying to be chosen to execute orders they did not realize had already been completed. (Years later, when inflows to index funds were setting volume records in 2015, the leading index fund managers experienced little or no market impact from their operations.)

According to William R. Grant, the widely respected vice chairman and former director of investment research for Smith Barney Harris Upham, in 1977:

> *The fiduciary responsibility of corporate directors is best discharged by assuring themselves that their pension funds are managed by those who practice successful active investment management rather than abdicating decisions to a mechanical structure just because it would have worked well over selected periods in the past or*

because it provides a comfortable release from potential legal anxieties. Those with a fiduciary responsibility cannot avoid decision making. There is no easy way or short cuts to success in any endeavor, especially investing.[51]

This view was soon rejected by Richard Posner and John Langbein in the *American Bar Foundation Research Journal*. They argued that indexing was actually the *only* way to fulfill fiduciary responsibilities.[52]

Resistance to indexing was not universal across the investment profession. William Gray, senior vice president of the Harris Bank in Chicago and an active user of indexing, asked in an article, "With all of this research, why aren't the results better known and appreciated?" His response, in part:

The labels have a clear "ivory tower" ring, perhaps conveying a notion of irrelevance to the practical world. ... Perhaps more important, some of the work has strongly suggested that certain elements of investment activity may not be particularly useful or not worth the cost. Can you think of any group that hasn't resisted the idea that their contribution may be worth less than they are being paid.[53]

John Casey, a pension consultant, added:

I feel sorry for a lot of these guys. They were trained to do things a certain way and have spent years working hard to do it in that familiar way. Now, suddenly, they're beginning to discover that what they've been doing all their lives hasn't worked and they've been doing everything the wrong way. Think of the psychological shock these guys must be going through. Sometimes I wonder how they manage to get up in the morning.[54]

• • •

Fifty years ago, it was realistic to believe that a careful analyst, experienced in investing and working in a good investment organization armed with good information and access to the computer power, could and would beat the market.

Forty years ago, I was so impressed by the large numbers of talented, driven people coming into investments that I had begun developing serious doubts about the chances of most managers being able to beat the market significantly and regularly and began to wonder whether active investing was a game worth playing.

Since then, I've had an extraordinarily privileged opportunity to get to know many of the leading investors all over the world and to work with them as a strategy consultant and confidential adviser. As I learned how capable many professional investors had become, my doubts about the chances of any of them consistently outperforming all the others after fees and costs have grown—and grown.

I've also become convinced that almost all investors choosing to pursue active investing will prove unable to identify managers who will meet the performance expectations they encourage or, after costs and adjustments for risk, earn the fees being charged over the long term.

Over these many years, the reasons behind my changing views have been accumulating. More than almost anyone else, thanks to the unusual opportunities that have come my way, I've been immersed in the hard evidence of changes in the structure and composition of the stock market that make almost all the important information available to almost all investors everywhere. I've also been immersed in the extraordinary increases in the quality and quantity of talent attracted to the persistent pursuit of superior price discovery—identifying the pricing errors of other experts (and doing so before still other experts can) and finding enough pricing errors to overcome the costs of portfolio operations and management fees.

In *Exit, Voice and Loyalty,*[55] Albert Hirschman explored the choices responsible people can make when their organization is failing. *Exit* means simply leaving. *Voice* means staying and arguing for a change in direction. *Loyalty* means staying and supporting the policies that are failing—and is a dead end. Exit has little effect, and voice, to be effective, must be forceful enough to be clearly heard.

Investment management has been my world for over 50 years and has provided me with a wonderful career; acquaintance with many bright, informed, interesting people; and many close friendships. So now, when the old ways that did work so well years ago—after so much change on so many dimensions—are no longer working because the markets have become so effective at price discovery, I've found that only one of Hirschman's three choices makes any sense: voice. I hope the hundreds of thousands of institutional investors who invest for many millions of individual investors *and* the millions of individual investors will—using the reasoning and techniques explored in the following chapters—take advantage of my privileged opportunities to see why almost all investors would be wise to index now.

As shown Figures 1.1 and 1.2, increasingly, investors are agreeing *and* joining the Index Revolution with increasing commitments to both mutual funds and index ETFs. So now let's turn to a deeper study of each of the main reasons for joining the Index Revolution, starting with the Big Four reasons to shift from active investing to indexing.

NOTES

1. Over the years, my services to the CFA program would include two years on a committee creating exam questions and four long weekends in Charlottesville grading exams and learning about the cost of unreadable handwriting, the importance of rereading your exam paper before turning it in to be sure you hadn't left out an essential "not," reading the questions carefully so you don't, however eloquently, answer the wrong question, and not spending so much time on one question that you didn't have time to answer all the others; chairing the continuing education committee when we designed a major publications program based on specific subject conferences; and twice serving on the profession's governing board, finally as chairman.

This position led to a challenging role during the difficult discussions that finally resulted in merging the Financial Analysts Federation, a highly political, money-losing, and weak confederation of 30 different and very independently run local societies across North America, with the CFA Institute, a single, integrated, international organization then known as the Association for Investment Management Research (AIMR). Members were all analysts or portfolio managers (no salesmen or stockbrokers were allowed) and had earned the CFA Charter. The CFA Institute's members had consistent values and aspirations, and it had strong finances—because members' employers typically paid the significant exam fees *and* the annual dues.

In 2011, during one of my six week-long trips to Vietnam that year, it was my privilege to award eight CFA Charters to aspiring young professionals in that still communist country. I was particularly pleased when LeViet Nga came up to receive her charter. We had worked together in Hanoi at Vietnam Partners, an investment firm. By then, there were over 100,000 CFAs around the world, and the nations with the largest number of candidates other than the United States were India and China. The CFA Institute was certainly fulfilling Ben Graham's vision of an international standard-setter for the investment profession. Ben Graham had proposed a QFA—Qualified Financial Analyst—certification in the 1950s. At that time, most analysts thought the idea absurd.

2. Excluding market facilitation trading by NYSE Specialists—a group who have since disappeared.

3. The research was led by Terrance O'Dean.

4. From Scantlin Electronics, Inc. My employers, the Rockefeller family, had helped finance Jack Scantlin's new company.

5. By 'Adam Smith,' the pen name of George J. W. Goodman.

6. "Will Success Spoil Performance Investing," *Financial Analysts Journal*, September–October 1968.

7. See Richard A. Brealey, *An Introduction to Risk and Return from Common Stocks* (Cambridge, MA: MIT Press, 1969), 5, 6; Eugene F. Fama, "The Behavior of Stock Practices," *Journal of Business,* January 1965, 34–105; and Michael C. Jensen, "Random Walks and Technical Theories: Some Additional Evidence," *Journal of Finance,* May 1970, 469–482.

8. James H. Lorie and Mary T. Hamilton, *The Stock Market: Theories and Evidence* (Homewood, IL: Richard D. Irwin, Inc., 1973), 100.

9. Ibid., 80.

10. Charles P. Jones and Robert H. Litzenberger, "Quarterly Earnings Reports and Intermediate Stock Price Trends," *Journal of Finance,* March 1970, pp. 143–148.

11. James H. Lorie and Victor Niederhoffer, "Predictive and Statistical Properties of Insider Trading," *Journal of Law and Economics,* April 1968, 35–53.

12. Michael C. Jensen, "The Performance of Mutual Funds in the Period 1945–64," *The Journal of Finance* 23, No. 2 (May 1968): 389–416.

13. Fischer Black, "Implications of the Random Walk Hypothesis for Portfolio Management," *Financial Analysts Journal* 27, No. 2 (March–April 1971): 19.

14. See Wharton School of Finance and Commerce, *A Study of Mutual Funds*, Reports of the Committee on Interstate and Foreign Commerce, 87th Congress, House Report 2274, 1962; and Jensen, "The Performance of Mutual Funds."

15. "Portfolio Operations," *Financial Analysts Journal,* September–October 1971, 36–46.

16. See, for example, *New Breed on Wall Street* by Martin Mayer, in which several dozen investment managers are profiled.

17. Mutual funds directly and pension funds by moving money out of bank trust departments into newly formed investment firms.

18. Later, Jay Light became dean of the Harvard Business School—and a member of Greenwich Associates' board of directors.

19. Called Wells Fargo Investment Advisors, it was entirely separate from the bank's trust department. Later acquired by Nikko, which was acquired by Barclays Global and renamed BGI, which was acquired by BlackRock and is now a major part of the world's largest investment management organization.

20. As a project for CFA Institute, Jim Vertin and I jointly organized and selected the salient articles in the long literature of investing, which we published in two volumes of "Classics." In addition to seminal pieces form the past, those two volumes also had all the core papers of Harry Markowitz, Paul Samuelson, Fischer Black, Myron Scholes, Milton Friedman, and others.

21. Jonathan R. Laing, "More Pension Funds Try to Tie the Market Instead of Beating It," *Wall Street Journal,* November 12, 1975.

22. Two potential entrants failed to reach the stage of actively offering index funds. American Express Investment Management

Company was liquidated before its intended mutual fund was offered, and Wells Fargo's Stagecoach Fund, which would have been a leveraged index fund, was withdrawn from the registration due to inadequate demand from investors.

23. George P. Williamson, Jr., "Illinois Bell Answers the Index Fund Call," *Pension & Investments,* June 23, 1976.

24. Michael Clowes, "Index Funds Nabbing a Growing Share of the Market," *Pension & Investments*, June 23, 1976.

25. A. F. Ehrbar, "Index Funds—an Idea Whose Time Is Coming," *Fortune* 93, No. 6 (June 1976): 146.

26. Laing, "More Pension Funds," 1.

27. Paul A. Samuelson, *Journal of Portfolio Management* 1 (Fall 1974): 17–19.

28. In early 2016, the 500 Index Fund's assets were over $400 billion.

29. Ehrbar, "Index Funds—an Idea Whose Time Is Coming," 146.

30. James Lorie, "Index Funds Are Important," at the A. G. Becker Conference.

31. Barbara A. Patocka, "Is Superior Money Management Possible?," *Pensions* 2, No. 4 (October 1972): 25.

32. Ibid., 27.

33. Jonathan R. Laing, "Bye Bye, Go-Go?" *The Wall Street Journal,* June 7, 1973, p. 1.

34. Robert Metz, "Most Banks Do Poorly on Pooled Funds," *The New York Times,* March 21, 1976.

35. Becker Securities 1975 Institutional Funds Evaluation Service.

36. "Index Funds and Index Matching," *Atlanta Economic Review.*

37. Paul A. Samuelson, "Challenge to Judgment," *The Journal of Portfolio Management,* Summer 1975, 18.

38. John K. Galbraith, *New York Times Book Review,* May 16, 1965, 34.

39. Thomas S. Kuhn, *The Structure of Scientific Revolutions* (Chicago, IL: University of Chicago Press, 1962), 157.

40. The poster was distributed by the Leuthold Group, a small division of a regional broker, Piper Jaffray & Hopwood.

41. Robert J. Cirino, "If Index Funds Are So Great, How Come So Little Pension Money Has Been Going into Them?" *Institutional Investor,* June 1977, 3.

42. Vartanig G. Vartan, "Why Indexing Frightens Money Managers," *New York Times,* October 3, 1976, 58.

43. David L. Babson, "Index Funds, Why Throw in the Towel?" *Weekly Staff Letter of David L. Babson & Co., Inc.,* December 18, 1975, 1.

44. Nancy Belliveau, "Much Ado About Index Funds," *Institutional Investor,* February, 1976, 23.

45. Roger F. Murray, "Index Funds: An Idea Whose Time Has Passed," *Pensions & Investments,* February 16, 1976, 19; and Charles D. Ellis, "The Loser's Game" *Financial Analysts Journal,* 1971. To my very happy surprise, the book that grew out of the *FAJ* article, *Winning the Loser's Game,* published by McGraw-Hill and soon to be in its seventh edition, has sold over 500,000 copies.

46. Barton M. Biggs, *Investment Strategy,* Morgan Stanley & Co., January 23, 1976, 1.

47. Belliveau, "Much Ado About Index Funds," 18.

48. Scudder, Stevens & Clark, *General Information Memorandum #45-1,* October 1, 1976, 3.

49. "Index Funds Remain Unruffled by S&P Addition," *Pensions & Investments,* August 2, 1976, 10.

50. Michael Clowes, "New York Funds' Trading Goes Unnoticed," *Pensions & Investments*, March 28, 1977, 1.

51. William R. Grant, *Predestination and Pension Funds*, memorandum published privately, Smith Barney, Harris Upham, February 1977.

52. John H. Langbein and Richard A. Posner, "Market Funds and Trust-Investment Law," *American Bar Foundation Research Journal,* No. 1, 1976, 1–34.

53. William S. Gray III, "Index Funds and Market Timing," *Trusts and Estates,* May 1976, 18.

54. Ibid., 35.

55. Published in 1970 by the president and fellows of Harvard College.

PART TWO

THE 10 GOOD REASONS TO INDEX

2

THE STOCK
MARKETS OF
THE WORLD
HAVE CHANGED
EXTRAORDINARILY

The stock markets of the world—and the world of investment management—have changed so much in so many ways that today's stock markets are almost totally different from the markets of 50 years ago. Scale. Speed. Technology. Information. Globalization. Innovation. Regulation. Institutions. Much more competition. These are powerful change forces that have been combining and compounding to change the realities of financial markets around the world—an extraordinary transformation that all investors should recognize and accept before they make decisions about how they will invest.

When anyone or anything has gone through many quantitative changes, they will probably experience important qualitative changes, too. Over the past half-century, major securities markets have gone through extraordinary quantitative and qualitative changes. Before considering the many ways their changes compound one another, let's recognize the extraordinary magnitude of each major contributing force in the overall transformation. Here are examples of 50 years of change:

- Trading volume of New York Stock Exchange listed stocks increased from 3 million a day to 5 billion, a change in volume of over 1,500 times.
- The dollar value of trading in derivatives rose from *zero* to more than the value of the "cash market."

- The investors executing this surging volume of trading have changed profoundly. Individual amateur investors did over 90 percent of all New York Stock Exchange (NYSE) trading 50 years ago. They *may* have read an article in *Forbes, Barron's, Business Week*, or a newspaper or taken advice from their busy broker, but they were market *outsiders*. They were not regular traders. They averaged less than one trade in a year, and almost half their purchases were AT&T common stock, then the most widely owned U.S. stock.

  Fifty years later, the share of trading by individuals has been overwhelmed by institutional and high-speed machine trading to over 98 percent. Today, the 50 most active (and ruthless) professionals—half of them hedge funds—do 50 percent of all NYSE listed stock trading, and the smallest of these 50 giants spends $100 million annually in fees and commissions buying information services from the global securities industry. These institutions are all market *insiders* who get the "first call"—and they know what to do with new information.

- Investment research from major securities firms in all the major markets around the world, produced by expert analysts of companies and industries, economists, political analysts, demographers, and geologists, amounts to an enormous volume of useful information. It is distributed almost instantly via the Internet to hundreds of thousands of analysts and portfolio managers who work in fast-response decision-making organizations worldwide.

- Competitors of all sorts and sizes all over the world operate out of vast trading rooms dominated by many large computer screens displaying multiple instantaneous data feeds processed by commercial and proprietary computer programs.

- Bloomberg machines, unheard of 50 years ago, now number over 320,000 and spew unlimited market and economic data virtually 24 hours a day.

- The population of CFAs (Chartered Financial Analysts) has gone from zero 50 years ago to 135,000, with over 200,000 more in the queue studying for the tough annual exams where pass rates are less than 60 percent.

- Algorithmic trading, computer models, and corps of inventive "quants" (quantitative analysts) were unheard of years ago. Today, they are major market participants.

- The Internet, e-mail, and blast faxes have created a revolution in global communications: instantaneous, worldwide, and accessible 24/7. We really are all in this together.

- National securities markets, once isolated, are increasingly integrated into one nearly seamless global megamarket operating around the clock and around the world. And this megamarket is increasingly integrating with and transforming bond markets and currency markets as well as the major markets for such commodities as oil, gold, and wheat.

- Regulations have changed to ensure simultaneous disclosure to all investors of all potentially important investment information. Since 2000 in the United States, the Securities and Exchange Commission's Regulation FD (Fair Disclosure) has required that *any* significant corporate information be made simultaneously available to *all* investors. (Years ago, such information—when proprietary—was central to successful active investing.) Regulation FD is a game "changer" that has effectively commoditized investment information from corporations.

- Hedge funds, acquisitive corporations, activist investors, and private equity funds have all—with different perspectives and different objectives—become major participants in price discovery in today's securities markets, now the world's largest and most active prediction market.

In combination, these major changes have been extraordinarily transformative. As Dorothy said to Toto, "We're not in Kansas anymore!"

Fifty years ago, I thought it was realistic to expect that an experienced investment leader could select a team of portfolio managers and analysts who could and would "beat the market." I still hold this belief about the prospects for active investors *back then.* But after a half-century of major, compounding, multidimensional change, it has become virtually impossible for all but a very few investment organizations to outperform the market after fees and costs over the long-term future. And even for most of those exceptional few, the risk-adjusted magnitude of potential success is too uncertain and too small in most cases to justify the commitment. This is particularly true if it distracts investors from the far more important and rewarding work of defining their important objectives, determining the investment policies most capable of achieving those objectives, *and* staying the course.

The past 10 years have accumulated undeniable evidence that almost all investors would do better to rely on indexing for their investment operations and concentrate their time and talent on tailoring investment policies to achieve their own specific objectives.

As markets continue to change, it is theoretically possible that so many active investors will convert to indexing that markets may again become relatively inefficient and active managers can be winners again. Maybe, but not likely. Here's why:

First, while index funds and index exchange-traded funds (ETFs) now approach 30 percent of stock market *assets,* their turnover is so small compared to that of active investors that they account for less than 5 percent of trading, and trading is what sets prices.

Second, the only way to reduce the competitive striving of active investment managers would be to make their work so unrewarding that they would decide to quit.

Given how highly compensated active managers are these days, it would take an awfully large drop in compensation to cause many active managers to leave the market.

Third, the crucial challenge for active managers is swift access to superior information. The combination of Regulation FD, lots of Bloombergs, and the Internet have made accurate information immediately available at minimal cost to literally every professional investor. And this is what makes it so very hard for any one firm to outperform the many other experts.

Open-to-all, well-regulated, and deep markets with accurate public prices are a major economic good. We—investors, companies, and workers—are all fortunate to have excellent markets. So long as this is our reality, like good water or freedom from fear or violence, shouldn't each individual or institution recognize and enjoy the advantages?

3

INDEXING OUTPERFORMS ACTIVE INVESTING

Beliefs are strong—particularly beliefs we *want* to believe in. That's why in most wars, people on both sides are sure they're right and why creationism is still taught in some states as an alternative theory to evolution, and why some people still resist climate change. So we should look at the facts because, as Churchill explained, "The facts are looking at us!"

The stunning reality is that most actively managed mutual funds fail to keep up with index funds that match those active funds' chosen benchmarks. The problem gets worse as the time period gets longer. (This is important because while they may change specific investments or managers, most investors will be continuously investing one way or another for the next 20, 30, or 40 years or even longer— and much longer when including the investing years of their heirs.) The point on low success rates is made dramatically in Table 3.1 based on data from Morningstar,[1] the most trusted independent evaluator of mutual fund performance.

Table 3.1 Active Funds' "Low Success Rate" by Category

Category	1-Year	3-Year	5-Year	10-Year
Large Blend	27.7%	27.8%	16.3%	16.6%
Large Value	36.5	34.6	19.6	33.7
Large Growth	49.3	18.9	11.9	12.2
Small Blend	50.2	34.9	32.8	24.7
Small Value	66.7	54.1	38.0	38.3
Small Growth	22.3	28.6	20.6	23.2
Foreign Large	63.6	47.6	44.7	33.9
Emerging Markets	63.0	55.9	61.2	42.3

Source: Morningstar. Data and calculations as of December 31, 2015.

Note particularly how low the "success rate" is over 10 years. Not even one-half of the mutual funds in any category match or beat their chosen index or benchmark. (The following data are shown after deduction of fees from all funds.) In three out of four categories, less than 35 percent of the funds match or keep up with the standards they aim to beat. This grim reality is the crux of the matter for serious investors: more than three out of four funds are losers.

At least as serious as the sizable shortfall, nearly half of mutual funds did not even survive for 10 years. Funds that were closed down or merged into other, better-performing funds over the decade, usually for poor performance, amounted to no less than:

- 40 percent of all large value funds.
- 48 percent of all large growth funds.
- 32 percent of all small value funds.
- 47 percent of all small growth funds.

Finally, Figure 3.1 shows there's a painful "sting in the tail" from funds that close: They tend to decline sharply during their last 12 to 18 months before being quietly buried, never again to be reported or even acknowledged. These abandoned orphans are essential parts of the whole truth that all investors need know and understand.

Figure 3.1 How Closed Funds Declined at Their End

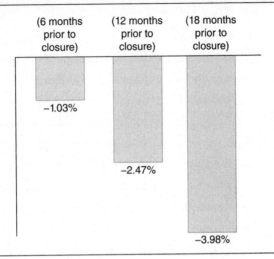

Sources: Vanguard calculations, using data from Morningstar, Inc.

Most investors will not recognize these data. As many might say, "The performance numbers I've seen are much more favorable than these. Something must be wrong." What's wrong is this: The way numbers are reported in advertisements and promotional materials gives investors a false "enhanced" impression of the capabilities and performance of active managers. Unfortunately, this deception is not accidental.

No law or regulation requires mutual fund organizations to keep reporting funds they no longer manage, nor are they required to report how many funds in their fund family have been closed or merged into a stronger fund in the same family. Nor is there any requirement to report the poor performance that preceded the closure or merger. As a result, many mutual fund families do what other mutual fund families do. In a race to the bottom—"All the other kids do it, Mom"—the poor and mediocre performers get deleted from the database as though they had never existed. Adding the deleted failures back into the record converts favorable claims to unfavorable evidence and flips the conclusion from active usually works over to active usually does not work.

Similar manipulations are fashioned by consultants retained by institutional investors to help select investment managers. When they drop a manager from their recommended lists, they usually delete all data on that manager. When they *add* a new recommended manager, they retroactively add that manager's favorable results for prior years. The deceptive result is a chart showing how "their" managers have outperformed.

Given the momentous changes in the competitive composition of the securities markets, thoughtful investors might correctly expect that it has been getting harder for most active investment managers to outperform their chosen benchmarks. The data in Table 3.2, which include results for funds that were merged or closed, confirm this pessimistic expectation. The trend over time is for larger and larger percentages of active managers to *under*perform their benchmarks each year. Only a relatively small minority have achieved success. In almost every category and in almost every year, active managers of mutual funds underperform their own chosen benchmarks.

Data from Morningstar, MSCI, CRISP, Standard & Poor's, and Vanguard report a similarly compelling pattern of serious shortfalls in category after category of equity funds. In the 10 years ending in 2015, 82 percent of "large-cap" funds, 94 percent of "large-cap growth" managers, 61 percent of "large-cap value" managers and 88 percent of "small-cap" funds had results below their chosen benchmarks (see Table 3.3). At least as concerning to serious long-term investors, more than 40 percent of the 2,080 different funds that were tracked at some time over the past decade have *disappeared*—usually through merger into another fund with similar objectives—and only one-third of funds have sustained their commitment to a particular investment focus style over the full 10 years.

Table 3.2 Annual League Table of Outperformance of Active Fund Managers

Fund Category	Benchmark Index	2000	2001	2002	2003	2004	2005	2006	2007	2008	2009	2010	2011	2012	2013	2014	2015
All Domestic Funds	S&P Composite 1500	40.5	54.5	59.0	47.7	51.4	44.0	67.8	48.8	64.2	41.7	57.6	84.1	66.1	46.1	87.2	74.8
All Large-Cap	S&P 500	36.9	57.6	61.0	64.6	61.6	44.5	69.1	44.8	54.3	50.8	61.8	81.3	63.3	55.8	86.4	66.1
All Mid-Cap	S&P MidCap 400	78.9	67.3	70.3	56.4	61.8	76.0	46.7	46.4	74.7	57.6	78.2	67.4	80.5	39.0	66.2	56.8
All Small-Cap	S&P SmallCap 600	70.7	66.4	73.6	38.8	85.0	60.5	63.6	45.0	83.8	32.2	36.0	85.8	66.5	68.1	72.9	72.2
Large-Cap Growth	S&P 500 Growth	16.0	87.5	71.8	44.7	39.5	31.6	76.1	31.6	90.0	39.1	82.0	96.0	46.1	42.7	96.0	49.3
Large-Cap Value	S&P 500 Value	54.5	20.6	39.4	78.5	83.2	58.8	87.7	46.3	22.1	46.2	34.7	54.3	85.0	66.6	78.6	59.1
Mid-Cap Growth	S&P MidCap 400	78.4	79.0	87.0	31.7	59.7	78.6	34.9	39.3	89.0	59.7	82.1	75.4	87.2	36.7	56.2	79.9
Mid-Cap Value	S&P MidCap 400 Value	94.8	55.8	74.3	81.9	63.6	71.8	38.4	56.1	67.1	47.8	71.8	64.9	76.2	45.3	73.6	32.4
Small-Cap Growth	S&P SmallCap 600 Growth	73.0	81.3	94.2	35.3	93.6	72.2	52.1	39.4	95.5	33.5	72.7	93.8	63.7	55.6	64.5	88.4
Small-Cap Value	S&P Small Cap 600 Value	74.4	48.7	37.5	49.3	77.5	46.0	77.0	39.9	72.5	26.3	51.8	83.0	61.8	79.0	94.3	46.6

Source: S&P Dow Jones Indicies LLC, CRSP. Data as of December 3, 2015. Outperformance is based on equal-weighted fund counts.

Table 3.3 Percentage of U.S. Equity Funds Outperformed by Benchmarks

Fund Category	Comparison Index	1-Year (%)	3-Year (%)	5-Year (%)	10-Year (%)
All Domestic Equity Funds	S&P Composite 1500	74.8	80.9	88.4	83.2
All Large-Cap Funds	S&P 500	66.1	75.8	84.1	82.1
All Mid-Cap Funds	S&P MidCap 400	56.8	61.6	76.7	87.6
All Small-Cap Funds	S&P SmallCap 600	72.2	81.7	90.1	88.4
All Multi-Cap Funds	S&P Composite 1500	73.6	79.6	88.6	88.3
Large-Cap Growth Funds	S&P 500 Growth	49.3	76.3	86.5	93.6
Large-Cap Value Funds	S&P 500 Value	59.1	78.7	82.1	31.00

Source: S&P Dow Jones Indices LLC, CRSP. Data as of December 3, 2015. Outperformance is based on equal-weighted fund counts.

Table 3.4, shows over a 10-year period, a stunning 40 percent of mutual funds were terminated within 10 years. In addition, only 36 percent of funds stayed on policy and maintained a consistent style of investing.

While the popular myth is that active investors should have a significant competitive advantage in less efficient markets such as small-cap stocks and emerging markets, hard data show little support for those beliefs. Contrary to the popular expectation that "this market is different," Table 3.5 shows that the rate of failure in international funds is similar. (A few small markets may be exceptions.)

Table 3.4 Survivorship and Style Consistency of U.S. Equity Funds Are Both Low

Fund Category	No. of Funds at Start	Survivorship (%)	Style Consistency (%)
10-Year			
All Domestic Funds	2,110	60.0	35.9
All Large-Cap Funds	672	56.4	39.1
All Mid-Cap Funds	355	60.6	30.0
All Small-Cap Funds	475	63.2	41.9
All Multi-Cap Funds	608	61.9	31.4
Large-Cap Growth Funds	204	49.0	35.3
Large-Cap Value Funds	200	66.5	48.5
Mid-Cap Growth Funds	171	51.5	32.8
Mid-Cap Value Funds	89	73.3	20.9
Small-Cap Growth Funds	184	54.9	44.6
Small-Cap Value Funds	88	75.0	36.4

Source: S&P Dow Jones Indices LLC, CRSP. Data as of December 3, 2015. Outperformance is based on equal-weighted fund counts.

In high-yield bonds, emerging-market debt, and other less efficient markets, analysis and issue selection appear to be rewarding, particularly in avoiding serious risk.) Many believe the "smart money" has moved into hedge funds or activist funds, but after fees and taxes, the overall results are far from encouraging, and given the number of terminations, the search for successful funds is seriously challenging, particularly after taxes.

Table 3.5 shows how many "international" funds lagged behind their chosen benchmarks over the past 10 years.

The specter of underperformance that now haunts active investing will not go away. It will get worse for a

Table 3.5 Percentage of International Funds that Lag Benchmarks

Fund Category	Benchmark Index	10-Year Percentage
Global	S&P Global 1200	79.2%
International	S&P International 700	84.1%
International Small-Cap	S&P Developed Markets Ex-U.S. SmallCap	58.1%
Emerging Markets	S&P/IFCI Composite	89.7%

Source: S&P Dow Jones Indices LLC, Morningstar. Data periods ending December 31, 2015. Past performance is no guarantee of future results.

profoundly ironic reason. History's largest, most capable, best-informed, and most highly competitive professional investors dominate today's stock market. So almost no one in this magnificent crowd can expect to outperform the others regularly *after* cost and fees. Active managers aren't failing to beat the market because they are not informed, skillful, expert, and diligent. Quite the opposite; they can't outperform the expert consensus of the other active managers after fees and costs with any consistency over time because so many competitors are so skillful, informed, hardworking, and so well armed with information and technology. That's why, as a percentage of their real value added, incremental fees for active management—as will be shown in the next chapter—are now *over 100 percent.*

Yet professional investors and the independent directors of actively managed mutual funds with fiduciary duties continue to refuse to accept the objective data or insist on looking past it. As the behavioral economist and Nobel Prize winner Daniel Kahneman quietly observes: "People can maintain unshakable faith in any proposition when supported by enough co-believers."[2]

Even if an active manager could magically know the facts of the future, that wouldn't be enough to be sure of adding value. The investor would also need to have a superior understanding of how other investors were discounting their anticipation of how still other active investors were discounting their expectation of these anticipations, and so on *ad infinitum.* No wonder market prices and "market sentiment" change so often in rapid, random deviations from uncertain central values. But that is just random noise—sound and fury signifying nothing.

• • •

To a large extent, the key to successful investing is simply avoiding common mistakes. That was the premise of my 1975 article "The Loser's Game," in which I combined the cold facts that performance investing was not working with a concept based on Simon Ramo's short book with this compelling title*: Extraordinary Tennis for the Ordinary Tennis Player.*[3] Ramo, a first-rate club tennis player, declared that there are two very different games called tennis. Both use the same court, balls, racquets, scoring, and dress code. However, the actual playing and the key to winning are *not* the same. They are opposite. A few superb players correctly play to win. All other players—if they aim to win matches—should play to *not lose.*

Most tennis players are not able to hit 130-mile-per-hour serves with great accuracy. If they try to hit hard serves, they will hit faults. If they try to drill a ball close to the line, all too many will go out. Ramo calculated that about 90 percent of professional points are won, while 90 percent of amateur points are lost. For most players, tennis is a loser's game, with the loser determining who is the eventual winner. So, for amateurs, the key to winning points, sets, and matches is to play well within your capabilities and not lose. To win, lose less than your opponent. Investing was a winner's game in the early 1960s, but due to the many major changes in the market, it became and will forever be a loser's game, where the winner makes fewer mistakes.

NOTES

1. Called the Active/Passive Barometer, it measures U.S. active managers versus their passive peers in each category using actual net-of-fees results (rather than an index, which is not investable).
2. Daniel Kahneman, *Thinking, Fast and Slow* (New York, NY: Farrar, Straus and Giroux, 2011).
3. Simon Ramo, *Extraordinary Tennis for the Ordinary Tennis Player,* 6th ed. (New York, NY: Crown Publishers, 1973).

4

LOW FEES ARE AN IMPORTANT REASON TO INDEX

My father taught lessons in a memorable way. In the late 1950s, we children came home at the end of a winter's Saturday afternoon of movies at the Warwick Theatre on Pleasant Street in Marblehead, Massachusetts, and Dad asked, "Enjoy the movies?"

"Yep."

"What'd you see?"

"John Wayne."

"What does the Warwick charge?"

"Twelve cents under 12 and 35 cents over 12."

Then Dad asked one of those questions that starts a lifetime of pondering: "Why?"

The easy answer was easy: "Because we're kids, Dad. And they charge only 12 cents so lots of kids will come." But easy answers wouldn't do, and Dad persisted, "Why does the Warwick charge only 12 cents when the truth is, they don't make *any* money showing movies?"

"Dad, is this a trick question?"

"No, it's not a trick question, but getting the right answer will take some careful thinking."

And that's how Dad got us to work it out with him that the folks at the Warwick were willing to show John Wayne movies at a loss because they were making a big profit selling Cokes and popcorn at stratospheric prices. Dad wanted us to learn to separate appearances from realities.

Several years later, Mom and Dad invited us to join them in New York City for dinner at a very special French restaurant named Cafe Chambord. As we examined the enormous menu, we couldn't help commenting on how wonderful the dinner would be—and how very expensive.

Then Dad asked another of his special questions: "How would you explain this fine restaurant's continuing in business if I told you something I happen to know: They don't make *any* profit selling this wonderful food?"

"Dad, is this a trick question?"

"No, it's not a trick question, but getting the right answer will take some careful thinking." And that's when we learned that the profits at a great restaurant are not from gourmet food, but from drinks—cocktails and wine. Dad was once again teaching us to think about the salient differences between appearance and reality in pricing.

The pricing of investment management services has been an exception for the past 50 years to the hallowed laws of economics.[1] Interestingly, this exceptional status—a status most buyers and sellers of investment services appear to assume has always been with us and will continue forever—may in fact be subject to change, even perhaps to substantial disruption. The early rumblings of a potential tectonic shift—not sudden, but forceful and inevitable—may be discernible even now.

These memories of Dad's teaching are relevant background for a personal confession. Until recently, I had missed the obvious reality: *Fees for investment management are not low.* They are high—very high.

The obvious came to me recently during an investment committee meeting as we listened to the well-known portfolio manager. He was talking about our being in partnership as manager and client, which certainly sounded appealing as the basis for a strong working relationship that had been developing over years of collegial efforts. By then, I had served on over a dozen investment committees and felt comfortable with the role and responsibilities of a committee member. I also believed that as clients, we were at least as responsible for fostering the quality of the relationship as was the manager. So *partnership* sounded right to me.

But, as I listened and looked at the numbers in our reports, I recalled the admonition of J. Richardson Dilworth, my boss at Rockefeller Brothers: "Always be sure you know who is the horse and who is playing Lady Godiva." As I looked at the data on investment returns—gross and net of fees—I finally saw the obvious. We were at best unusual "partners." Our endowment fund was putting up all the capital and taking all the market risks while the manager was getting a steady and substantial fee—the difference between gross and net returns. What dramatized the difference between us as partners was the grim reality that the manager had recently been underperforming, so our endowment was absorbing all the losses while the manager was continuing to collect full fees. Even averaged over many years—which showed a modest outperformance relative to the market—the manager was accumulating a large part of the total benefits of superior performance. Our endowment was performing the role of the horse: the manager was Lady Godiva.

Framing—the way we describe and see something—can make a major difference. So it has been with investment management fees. For years, investors and investment managers have both described fees with one four-letter word and one number: "only 1 percent." When stated as a percentage of *assets*, fund fees do look low—a little over 1 percent for mutual funds and half of 1 percent for separate accounts of institutional investors. But take a look from a different perspective and you'll never again think that fees are low—or that fees can be fairly described as "only 1 percent."

Let's do the math. Since you already have your assets, the right way to quantify investment fees is not as a percentage of the *assets* you have, but as a percentage of the *returns* that the investment manager produces. This simple first step into reality changes fees from a low "only 1 percent" to (assuming the consensus of 7 percent future returns on equities) a substantial 14 percent. This surely warrants deleting the four-letter word *only.* And that leap of insight turns out to be just the first toward a full understanding of investment management fees.

The second step is to recognize that all investors have alternatives. In their plain vanilla form, index funds consistently provide investors with the market rate of return at the market level of risk, and both have fees at a low "commodity" cost of around 10 basis points—one-tenth of 1 percent.

In intermediate microeconomics courses, we learn that all prices are relative to value, and the relative value of every good or service can be compared through prices to the relative value of every other good or service. In investment management, all investors have alternatives: alternatives by *degrees* (one active manager versus many others) and alternatives by *kind* (active versus index). The fees versus value of active investment management can and should be compared to the fees versus value of the low-cost commodity alternatives now so widely available, index funds and exchange-traded funds (ETFs).

Since all investors can invest via index funds and ETFs, any investor considering active investing will want to compare incremental returns with incremental fees. Since index funds and ETFs are widely available at 10 basis points and active mutual funds' fees are typically 100 basis points or more, the true cost of active investing is the *incremental fee* above indexing as a percentage of the *incremental return* above indexing. If the incremental return from active management after fees (and after adjusting for risk and uncertainty) were significantly higher than indexing after fees, investors might well decide that active management was good value for the money. For example, if there were an active mutual fund that beat the market over the long term *before* fees by 200 basis points (or two full percentage points), that might justify a fee of 1 percent, or 90 basis points above an index fund. That incremental 0.9 percent fee, however, would amount to *45 percent* of the active fund's 2.0 percent incremental return over an index fund—with clients putting up all the capital and taking all the risks. In practice, however, no manager of a major mutual fund has been beating the market by 200 basis points.

Now, being less obviously optimistic—but still highly hopeful—if a long-only manager charging "only 1 percent" were 110 basis points ahead of the market before fees, the real fee as a percentage of *incremental value added* (1.10 percent − 0.10 percent) would be 100 percent. That's why sensible investors should consider fees charged by active managers as the incremental fee's percentage of any risk-adjusted incremental returns above indexing. Thus, correctly stated, management fees for active management are remarkably *high.* Actually, the grim reality in markets all around the world is that a majority of active managers, after fees, fall short of the index they chose as their target to beat, so for those managers, incremental fees as a percentage of incremental returns are *over* 100 percent—or infinity.

Over a typical 12-month period, randomly selected for fairness, 60 percent of fund managers fall short of their own benchmarks. Since 12 months is much too short a period for evaluating a complex continuous process such as investment management, look at the record over a longer term. Over a decade, some 70 percent of mutual funds fall short of their benchmarks. Importantly, those that fall short do so, on average, by one and a half times as much as the winners get ahead. If the period for evaluation is doubled to 20 years—with caution flags up because the sample of mutual funds surviving 20 years is small—the percentage of funds falling short rises to 80 percent.[2] These data have been corrected for the obvious biases by adding back all funds no longer included in the database at the end of the period and deleting all "late date" retroactive data from funds that weren't available at the beginning of the period.

Can active investment managers continue to thrive on the assumption that clients won't figure out the reality that, compared to the readily available indexing alternative, fees for active management are so high?

Increasing fees have been *one* part of a little noticed duality. As fees were increasing, the value added by active investment managers has been declining, as shown in Chapter 3, for the many reasons detailed in Chapter 2. A substantial majority of active managers were underperforming their chosen benchmarks. Worse, it is virtually impossible to use past results for investors to predict which managers will achieve superior future results— with one exception: managers that charge low fees rather consistently do better than high-fee managers.

Pricing, as we learned in our introductory courses in economics, is *a,* if not *the,* vital factor in free markets. Price is where supply and demand curves meet and where free markets clear to the benefit of all buyers and sellers, so price drives progress. To understand the pricing of investment management services, it helps to know a little history.

In the early decades of the twentieth century, many trusts—particularly in Boston—having been created in law firms, were supervised by lawyers serving as trustees. Traditionally, lawyers were compensated by hourly fees, so the same practice was applied to trust administration, which involved such activities as payments to beneficiaries, collecting interest and dividends, filing tax returns, and overseeing trust investments. In Boston, the leading law firms often had units that specialized in investment matters, and income from trust administration and investment services provided a pleasant continuing income for retired former partners. Over time, some Boston trustees who did not have a general law practice concentrated entirely on trusts and investments.

One Boston trust and investment firm that did not have a law practice firm, Scudder, Stevens & Clark, came to the view in the early 1930s that hourly fees were not entirely appropriate since some trusts were very large and others rather small. The partners of the firm took the thoughtful position that fees, particularly for investment services, should be, in some sensible way, proportionate not to time but, rather, to the size of the investment portfolio. But should the fee be based on assets or on dividends? Given the difficulty of the question, the partners of that firm decided on a blend of both. A few years later, with the Depression in full force and the stock market down substantially, they decided it was not really fair to clients to base fees even partly on dividends, which were holding up, and switched to fees based entirely on assets. Clients commended this decision as evidence of professional integrity and recommended the firm to their friends and relatives.

Though they never do, every investment manager should celebrate that day with song, feasts, and much dancing. Changing the basis for fees from hours to assets would, in time, transform the economics of investment management. What had previously been at best a modestly compensated *profession* would, in time, become the world's most highly paid professional *business.*

Casual observers should be reminded that age is not nearly so career limiting in investment management as in other highly paid financial fields. Most investment bankers and traders retire voluntarily by age 50; most commercial banks have a fixed retirement age of 65; but investment managers often continue well into their 70s and some into their 80s.[3] In addition, many investment managers find opportunities on the side to invest their personal account in unusually attractive investments. While these extra opportunities do not affect the fees charged to clients, they do increase the overall compensation of investment managers.

Years ago, to protect widows and orphans, New York and other states set limits on the fees that bank trust departments could charge. These explicit fees were low, typically one-tenth of 1 percent per year. But banks, before the coming of negotiated commissions in the 1970s, found a back-door way to increase their income from trust activities. Banks, of course, earn profits by lending money, and if the Federal Reserve requires commercial banks to hold reserves equal to, say, 20 percent of loans made, a bank can lend five times its stable demand deposits. Brokers, in the ordinary course of their operations, held large cash balances. Deposited at a bank, those accounts enabled the bank to lend and earn interest on five times as much.

Both brokers and bankers knew the economic value of stable deposits, so naturally, a sophisticated bartering practice developed. Brokers would keep large deposits at a bank, and that bank's trust department would transact enough brokerage business to generate New York Stock Exchange (NYSE) commissions equal to, say, 6 percent of the broker's balances. Both banks and brokers knew the going rates, and both sides closely monitored the activity and the ratio of commissions to balances. A large fraction of the imputed income from brokers' balances would be credited within the overall banking organization to the trust division. Still, even with the two revenue streams—fees and compensating balances—investment management was at best only a marginal business and no great place for a career.

A major change was coming—but by stages. First, the volume of trading on the NYSE by institutional investors kept increasing while brokerage commissions stayed fixed at a set rate per 100 shares, no matter how large the total order. The big trust divisions of New York City banks—investing for clients in blue-chip stocks covered by their own research departments—had little use for Wall Street research and little need for brokers to risk their firm's capital in block trading. So they were particularly aggrieved to be paying high commissions for transactions of 5,000- or 20,000-share working orders that were so easy and so lucrative for brokers.

Demand creates supply, and Weeden & Company, a "third-market" firm, came to the rescue by offering to execute orders in listed stocks *off* the exchange at much lower commission charges. An early and major customer was the trust and investment division of Morgan Guaranty Trust, the largest and most blue-blooded trust operation. Since Morgan saw the Weeden arrangement as not fundamentally different from the well-established—and undisclosed to customers—reciprocity arrangements involving stockbrokerage commissions and stable deposit balances, it took the view that its customers were no worse off if they continued to pay the normal full commission. So the bank was "entrepreneurially entitled" to keep the difference between full NYSE commissions and the lower rates charged by Weeden. While keeping accurate records must have been a tedious chore for the clerks working in the back office or "cage" at banks and brokers, the trade-by-trade differential accumulated annually into amounts that became an important, even necessary part of the economics of the great bank's trust operations. As negotiated commissions came into the market, the special arrangement with Weeden came to an end. To keep its trust operations profitable, Morgan needed an alternative source of revenue.

In 1972, Morgan Guaranty stunned the investment world with an extraordinary announcement: beginning with the new year, institutional clients would be charged a significantly higher fee for investment management services: one-quarter of 1 percent. The immediate consensus was clear: Morgan Guaranty had made an enormous blunder! Large clients, particularly pension funds, would *never* accept such a fee increase. Despite its prestige and capabilities, Morgan Guaranty was sure to lose many accounts, particularly the largest accounts. Other managers, enthusiastically anticipating a bonanza, scrambled to capture as much of the departing business as they could.

All were disappointed. Morgan Guaranty did not lose lots of accounts. It lost one. One midsize account— period. Like the dog that did not bark in the Sherlock Holmes story, the unexpected silence sent a loud and clear message to investment managers. The same message was confirmed by the in-depth annual research conducted by Greenwich Associates. Out of two dozen criteria by which a new investment manager would be selected or the numerous possible reasons for terminating a manager, the *least* important to pension and endowment fund executives, year after year, was always the same: low fees. (Note that, in contrast, Morningstar, with all its data, cites low fees as the single best indicator of superior results.)

Thus began nearly a half century of persistent fee increases, facilitated by client perceptions that fees—if the right manager were chosen—would be comfortably exceeded by incremental returns. Even today, despite extensive evidence to the contrary, both individual and institutional investors typically expect their chosen managers to produce significantly higher than market returns. That perception, so very different from actual experience, may explain why fees have seemed low.

Even better than low fees not being required, higher fees were, ironically, seen as a clear sign of superiority. "You wouldn't choose a brain surgeon because he was cheaper, would you?" was the oft-repeated dismissal of the foolish idea that any sensible fund executive would select an investment manager on the trivial basis of a low fee.

A new group of competitors entered the fray during the 1960s. Some were stockbrokerage firms that had successfully established themselves as superior providers of investment research to major institutional investors. They soon began offering their services directly—as investment managers—to pension funds and endowments. Their terms were compelling: because they were brokers and therefore would naturally be executing most buy and sell orders through their own operations, they would charge a nominal fee of one-half of 1 percent or even 1 percent—but would deduct from this fee half of any commission charges. The happy result: deductions would almost always exceed nominal charges, so the real cost to the client would be zero.

For a zero net charge, a pension fund would get the individual attention of an agile team of bright young portfolio managers who lived, worked, and spoke with the top analysts every day, so communications were swift, direct, and fully nuanced. Being stockbrokers, these units saw effective selling as a positive strength, not as a demeaning compromise of high professional standards. While actually charging zero fees, these firms, aggressively seeking business all over the country, established the fee of 0.5 percent as the pricing norm for institutional accounts in the world's largest, most active institutional market for investment management services.

Indifference to fees in the 1960s and 1970s was not naïve. The aggressive, research-intensive new firms specializing in institutional portfolio management were, as performance measurement firms like A. G. Becker kept reporting, substantially outperforming the market *and* the established bank managers. Superior investment performance reduced the contributions needed to fund pension obligations, and this increased the sponsoring corporation's current earnings, often significantly. Corporate executives spoke of pension investing as a new profit center. Through the 1960s and 1970s, if it took paying fees of one-half of 1 percent to get 3 to 5 percent higher rates of return for a pension fund, the wisdom of paying up seemed self-evident.

Gradually, mutual fund companies, banks, and insurance companies organized special-purpose institutional units (often as separate subsidiaries of holding companies) and reset fees at higher levels than previously thought possible: typically that same one-half of 1 percent. While these were clearly higher than past fees, pension clients were not distressed: they were actually delighted to see their traditional service providers "modernizing" themselves to concentrate on institutional investing. As a strategy consultant to investment managers from 1972 to 2000, I witnessed this process of explaining fee increases many times and never observed a negative reaction by the clients of any manager.

Context matters. Surely, one major reason active managers were able to raise fees was a record long run of high-double-digit stock market returns. With clients' attention focused on the opportunities to do even better, would anyone be unwilling to share some of the bounty with the managers delivering such splendid results, particularly when everyone else seemed to be going along? Another reason is grounded in behavioral economics: investors have high hopes for the successes of their own managers. As Figure 4.1 shows, institutional fund executives—who collectively use almost all major managers—expected *their* particular managers to achieve results clearly far above the norm. On average, they expected their managers to beat the market by an astounding 100 basis points. Since over 1,000 pension and endowment funds collectively retain the services of virtually *all* managers—and hardly any investment managers regularly outperform the market by 100 basis points—this is, of course, a statistical impossibility. But it helps explain why high fees have held up. Another reason: fees for hedge funds and private equity funds are much higher. And, finally, nobody ever actually p*ays* the managers' fees by signing a check for hundreds of thousands of dollars. Fees are conveniently and quietly deducted by the manager from the assets being managed. Out of sight, out of mind.

Figure 4.1 Fund Executives Expect Their Managers to Out-perform *After* Fees

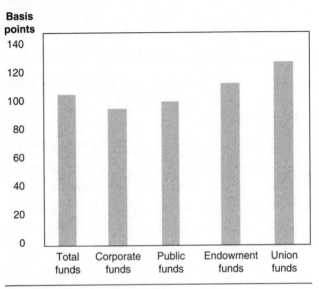

Source: Greenwich Associates' 41st annual study of institutional investors in 2015.

The unusual pricing phenomenon continued, even accelerated, as a new group of expert intermediaries entered the market as consultants to corporate and public pension funds and endowments on manager selection. Of course, the fees paid to these advisers added to the cost structure for active investment management. So, too, did the attendant costs of changing managers more frequently on the consultants' recommendations. Other factors have also added to costs. With advice from selection consultants, pension funds did not "bunch up" their plan assets with a few mega-managers to take advantage of sliding fee schedules. Rather, they increased the number of specialist managers working on their accounts— even though this meant higher fees—hoping that with many managers, each managing smaller accounts, the overall fund would benefit.[4]

Beginning in the 1980s, new forms of investment management with almost inevitably higher fee structures came into the institutional investment market: hedge funds and private equity firms. Originally known as leveraged buyout firms, they repositioned and renamed themselves after the 1990 book *Barbarians at the Gate* showed how ruthlessly aggressive these firms could be.

Fee escalation was also visible at mutual funds. When Massachusetts Investors Trust, America's first open-end mutual fund, was organized in 1924, its fee was set at 6 percent of the investment income, which was then the current bank rate for trustees. That was cut to 3.3 percent in 1949 or, as a percentage of assets, to 0.19 percent.

The lift-off in mutual fund fees was at least coincident with an obscure Ninth Circuit Court of Appeals decision in 1958 on the legality of the sale of a company managing a few small mutual funds. At issue was whether a company with fiduciary agreements to manage mutual funds "in the sole interest of the fund shareholders" could sell itself. The Securities and Exchange Commission (SEC) opposed the transaction vigorously, saying trafficking in management contracts would follow. But the U.S. Supreme Court declined to review the lower court's decision. By the early 1970s, one management company after another had either been sold or gone public. With a typical price-earnings ratio of 15, the pressure to increase profits by raising fees was intense, particularly on managers with large shareholdings.

Massachusetts Investors Trust's expense ratio, still 0.19 percent of assets in 1968, was doubled to 0.39 percent in 1976 when the trustees formed and took public the management company. The fee was almost doubled again to 0.75 percent in 1994. From this level, fees rose by nearly one-third to 0.97 percent in 1998 and by another 20 percent to 1.20 percent in 2003—equal to 80.4 percent of trust income. Dollar fees had risen by a stunning 36 *times* as assets increased only seven times. As it turned out, those fee increases were not at all unusual in the fund industry.[5]

In 1980, the SEC agreed to allow mutual fund managers to charge a new kind of fee, called by its specific enabling regulation 12(b)-1. These marketing fees, typically 0.2 percent to 0.3 percent of assets, are charged every year to investors in the funds that impose them, on the theory that the fee will motivate the mutual fund's selling broker to encourage all investors in the fund to be patient and so to continue longer term with the same fund. In theory, the investment manager should not have to maintain as large a cash position to cover possible redemptions and so should be able to stay focused on longer-term, presumably better, investing.[6]

The subtle skill with which language can be used is illustrated in this sentence from the Investment Company Institute's web site, with bracketed translations added: "12(b)-1 fees enable [oblige] investors to pay indirectly [in ways they do not recognize] for some or all of the services they receive [whether wanted or not] from financial professionals."

The next product-based change in fees came with indexing. Here, classic price competition between index providers came into play, and large funds were soon getting fees below 10 basis points (0.10 percent of assets). But not all index funds have followed suit. Since one large-cap index is nearly identical to another large-cap index, it is curious that in the retail markets, some index fund managers still charge fees up to "only 1 percent" and even higher for their index funds.

Some of the ways investment management organizations present their fees are disconcertingly deceptive. Mutual funds often report management fees separately from 12(b)-1 fees, so only a knowing investor would realize they are all part of the total cost. When the Investment Company Institute reports the long-term trend in mutual fund fees, it shows a graph of clearly declining fees without explaining that fee structures for actively managed funds have, overall, changed little, but as assets of funds increased, the incremental fees are slightly lower so while average fees have indeed been slightly lower, fee schedules have actually *increased* slightly over the same years. The fees in the graph are a blend of active and index fund fees. The main reason overall fees *appear* to trend lower over time is that low-cost index funds have been taking significantly increasing market share.

If the upward trend of fees and the downward trend of prospects for "beat the market" performance wave a warning flag for investors—as they certainly should—objective reality will cause all investors who have been believing investment management fees are low to reconsider.[7] Seen in the right perspective, active management fees are *not* low. Fees are high—very high—except for index funds.

NOTES

1. Another exception may be brain surgeons' fees for major operations. Yet another exception may be found on wine lists at fine restaurants frequented by hedge fund managers and IPOed tech whizzes who may select wines by the price. Sardonic sommeliers have been known to reprice a few expensive wines at deliberately inflated prices to attract the attention of customers with a private need to prove they can afford what they assume is "the very best."

2. Data provided by Vanguard.

3. Phil Carret, founder one of the first mutual funds, Pioneer Fund, worked a five-day week until age 100; Roy Neuberger, cofounder of Neuberger Berman, until age 94; and Irving Kahn continued to work at Kahn Brothers Group, Inc., four days a week to age 106. Warren Buffett and Charlie Munger, we all hope, will outlast them all.

4. Some pension funds attempted to shift from flat fees to performance fees, and some were able, at least briefly, to make a partial shift. But many managers successfully resisted that shift. The

SEC requires performance fees to be symmetrical (the penalty for missing the target must be the same as the reward for beating it). Fund executives also resisted, not wanting to pay more when they felt they had wisely selected winning managers and knowing they would find not paying the full fee small solace if a manager performed poorly. Vanguard, which uses many external managers for various funds, has agreed to performance-based fees with several of its managers with positive results. Fidelity may be unique in using performance fees on many of its mutual funds, a practice complementary to its culture and its commitment to performance investing. But these are exceptions.

5. One large mutual fund organization now cheerfully tells prospects for its advisory service, "Your fee will be only 1 percent." When a client looks more closely, however, the real fees total over 2 percent. When challenged, the salesman cheerfully responds, "Oh, that's just because of the fees for the individual mutual funds we use in this special service."

   Managers differ in the way they do or do not disclose or give credit to clients for fees earned through stock lending or how they charge for foreign exchange in international portfolios or how they allocate commissions in exchange for sales of the mutual funds they manage. The SEC's expansive interpretation of Section 28(e) allows payment in brokerage commissions for investment research and for Bloomberg terminals.

6. One particular charm of 12(b)-1 fees is that they continue indefinitely and can be passed along to a partner—perhaps a daughter or son who works with the parent for a few years and then takes

over entirely or on a 50-50 split. For a family, the amounts can be impressive. It would not be particularly unusual for the 12(b)-1 fees "earned" by a capable salesperson to reach $200,000 or even $400,000 annually, an unusually attractive "annuity."

"Revenue sharing" or paying brokers to emphasize particular funds is easier for funds that charge investors higher fees and so have more to share.

7. The U.S. Labor Department's announcement in February 2012 that it will require more disclosure of fees to 401(k) sponsors and participants may help some to do so.

5

INDEXING MAKES IT MUCH EASIER TO FOCUS ON YOUR MOST IMPORTANT INVESTMENT DECISIONS

Driving Mom and Dad home to Marblehead on Boston's North Shore after graduation ceremonies at Yale, I was staying at or just below the speed limit and carefully keeping an ample distance behind the other cars. Cruising quietly along the Mass Pike, I was slightly surprised by Dad's saying, "Somehow, at this time of year, I would have expected the moon to be on our left." Why the phases of the moon might be on his mind, I had no idea. I reminded Dad that the lunar month was only 28 days long and that the axis of the earth's rotation shifted with the seasons so, of course, the moon was seen in many different positions in the evening sky during the year.

Dad seemed satisfied by my erudition and we lapsed back into silence, making good time because traffic was light. My driving speed was fine, we had plenty of gas, and nobody was hungry or needed a pit stop. Then I saw a large green sign with white lettering: ALBANY 60 MILES. Focused on operating the car smoothly, I had just wasted an hour driving in the wrong direction!

Something similar happens to many investors. The fascinating short-term *operational* decisions all too often distract us from the central *policy* decisions that, over time, can make the most difference in our investment results and should be every investor's primary focus. The curse of active investing is not simply that it reduces returns, which it usually does, but that, with so much complexity, it diverts our attention from the profoundly important long-term investment policy decisions on which all investors should concentrate their time, energy, and thought.

Indexing helps investors succeed because indexing simplifies everything. Investors no longer have to monitor or worry about—or react to—the changing prices of specific stocks or keep up to date with short-term developments in companies and industries or the economy or all the interactive complexities. You can skip all those disconcerting details and you won't have to worry about the active manager losing his enthusiasm or "edge" or the fund being in the wrong sector of the market or your fund growing too large for market maneuverability and getting "too big to excel" or your fund management company selling out to a giant insurance company or any of a host of other troubles. These things happen all the time, which is why there's so much turnover in the Top 10 or Top 20 lists of managers as measured by their number of institutional client relationships, which should, of course, be very stable. (Of the 10 leading managers in 1972, only one, J. P. Morgan, remained in the Top 10 in 1999, and only one, T. Rowe Price, returned to the top in 2015.)[1]

Each investor is unique. That's why it is important that indexing enables each of us to concentrate on our core values and your personal long-term investment objectives. Investors who accept the challenge and the opportunity will shift their emphasis from reliance on the day-to-day craft of active investing and turn to the professional service of investment counseling—and shift from almost inevitably losing a little here and a little there to assured long-term winning.

Active investing can be interesting and exciting, but we all owe it to ourselves to remember that investing is not just a recreational game, it is serious business. Fortunately, there is another kind of serious "game" in investing, a game we *all* can win because victory doesn't depend (like boxing) on beating others, but (like golf) on mastering ourselves.

Everyone likes to succeed in investing. Millions of investors depend on investment success to ensure their financial security in retirement, to provide for their children's education, or to enjoy better lives. Schools, hospitals, museums, and colleges depend on successful investing of their endowments to fulfill their important missions. When investment professionals help investors define and achieve their particular realistic long-term objectives, investment management is a noble profession. The accumulating evidence, however, is that investors are suffering serious shortfalls. Part of the problem is that investors make mistakes. But they are not alone. Investment professionals need to recognize that much of the real fault lies not with their clients, but with themselves, the unhappy consequence of systemic errors. Let me explain.

For all its amazing complexity, the field of investment management really has only two major parts. One is the profession—doing what's best for investment clients—and the other is the business—doing what's best for investment managers. As in other professions, such as law, medicine, architecture, and management consulting, there is a continuing struggle between the values of the profession and the economics of the business. For investment managers to be really successful, they must retain the trust of clients *and* build a good business, and in the long run, the latter always depends on the former.

While the investment profession, like all learned professions, has many unusually difficult aspects that require great skill—and investing gets more complex almost daily—it, too, has just two major parts. One part is the increasingly difficult task of somehow combining imaginative research and astute portfolio management to achieve superior investment results by outsmarting the increasing number of professional investors who now dominate the markets and collectively set the prices of securities. As a result of a long-term transformation from an amateur's market to today's professional market, this is becoming more and more unlikely. Most investors are not beating the market; the market is beating them.

Difficulty is not always proportional to importance. In medicine, carefully washing one's hands has proven to be second only to antibiotics in saving lives. Fortunately, the second and more valuable part of what investment professionals do is the less difficult: investment counseling. Experienced professionals can help each client think through the sensible investment program most likely to achieve his or her own realistic long-term objectives *within* his or her own tolerance for various risks—variations in income, changes in the market value of assets, constraints on liquidity, and so on—and then help each client stay with that sensible investment program, particularly when markets seem full of exciting "this time it's different" opportunities or are fraught with threats. Success in this work is neither simple nor easy but is much easier than success in active investment management. And with new tools available to investment professionals,[2] investment counseling is getting easier even as active investing is getting steadily harder.

With remarkable irony, those devoting their careers to active investment management have unintentionally created three problems for themselves. Two are errors of commission with increasingly serious consequences. The third is an even graver error of omission. Unless practitioners change their ways, this troika of errors will harm the profession that has been so intellectually and financially rewarding to so many.

The first error of commission is that investment professionals have falsely defined their professional mission to clients and prospective clients as beating the market. In today's intensively competitive securities markets, most managers fall short. As we see in Chapter 3, identifying managers who will be the future winners is notoriously difficult, and the rate of subsequent failure of past market leaders is high. The grim reality of this first error of commission is that active managers continue selling what most have not delivered and realistically cannot and will not deliver: consistent beat-the-market investment performance. Sadly, most descriptions of performance do not even mention the most important aspect of investing: risk. Nor do the "performance" data adjust for taxes, particularly the high taxes on short-term gains that come with the now normal 60 to 80 percent annual portfolio turnover.[3] Nor is it comforting to see the details of how clients, both individuals and institutions, turn negative toward their investment managers after a few years of underperformance and switch to managers with a "hot" recent record. The sad result is that investors time and again buy *after* a fund's best results have been recorded and sell out *after* the worst performance is over. Thus, they position themselves for another round of buy-high, sell-low dissatisfaction and actually obliterate roughly one-third of their funds' actual long-term returns.[4] (Many individuals who actively manage their own investments notoriously do even worse.)[5] Unfortunately, this costly behavior is encouraged by advertising specific funds clearly selected because their good recent results—over carefully selected time periods—look better than some competitors' or benchmarks. Since most fund management families have many different funds, they will almost always have at least a few "documented winners."

Although over 80 percent of the investment committees of sponsors of pension plans and 401(k) options rate themselves "above average" on investment expertise, the average managers they fire go on to achieve slightly higher returns over the next few years than the managers they hire.[6] This switching behavior is costly. In selecting new managers, individual investors usually rely on fairly recent past performance even though studies of mutual funds show that for 9 out of 10 deciles of past performance, future performance is virtually random. Only one decile's past results have predictive power: the worst or 10th decile—apparently because only high fees and chronic incompetence have reliably repetitive impact on a manager's results.

The second error of commission by managers is allowing the values of the profession to become increasingly dominated by the economics of the business. Compared to 50 years ago, investment managers live in nicer homes, drive fancier cars, take more interesting vacations, and decorate their larger homes and offices with more remarkable paintings and sculptures. Private planes and "name it for me" philanthropy are not unknown. It is at least possible that the talented, competitive people attracted to investment management have, however unintentionally, gotten so caught up in competing for the tangible prizes that they are not asking potentially disruptive questions about the real value of their best efforts. Consider the main ways that the profitability of active investment management has increased over the past 50 years.

- Assets managed, with only occasional short pauses, have risen over sixfold.
- Fees as a percentage of assets have multiplied more than four times.

The combination has proven powerful. Meanwhile, costs have been relatively stable, so profits have increased rather greatly. With profits multiplied, not only has individual compensation flourished, but enterprise values are way up. Investment management organizations have become prime acquisition targets for giant financial service organizations such as banks, insurers, and securities dealers and the payouts to sellers have also become large, unless you think $1 billion for a first-generation service proprietorship is *not* large. When they choose to remain independent, some firms go public and others stay private, but they all recognize that they have become sizable, highly profitable businesses and so manage themselves appropriately.

As investment management organizations have been getting larger, business managers have increasingly displaced investment professionals in senior leadership positions. Business disciplines focus the attention of those with strong career ambitions on increasing profits, which is best achieved by increased asset gathering or sales, even though investment professionals know that expanding assets usually works against investment performance. At large financial service conglomerates, senior executives' judgments of division-by-division results tend to be profit focused rather than investment focused. The bigger the organization, the more likely it is that the focus of senior management will be on increasing business profits more than investment returns.

The basic trend of stock market prices is clearly upward. In the past, they have risen at more than twice the rate of the overall economy. Add to this strong underlying growth in assets, the positive impact of incremental sales to current clients, and the benefits of entering new markets with established products and developing new products for sale to established clients, and the annually compounding upward trend easily rises well above 10 percent. A service business that can grow at over 10 percent requires almost no capital at risk and can expand extensively while enjoying wide profit margins is, as Mae West said, "Wunnerful!" In a situation like this, what would any red-blooded business manager do? Would he not recognize the high margins on incremental assets and drive to gather assets, sell what is selling, and build the business?

At investment firms around the world, the two most important internal organizational changes have *not* been in improving investment research or in upgrading portfolio management. They have been in expanding new business development (to get more business when performance is favorable) and in augmenting relationship management (to keep more business longer, even when performance is unfavorable). These changes respond primarily to the realities of the business as a business, not to the needs of the profession as a profession or to the needs of clients as investors. When business dominates, it is not the friend of investment performance. Successful asset gathering eventually tends to overburden an organization's professional capacities for superior investing. In addition, actions aiming to increase profits such as cost controls, fee increases, and drives for greater productivity increase the chances that the organization's professional results will suffer.

The third error, an error of omission, is particularly troubling. In addition to the two errors of commission—accepting beat-the-market performance as the best measure of the profession and focusing attention on business achievements rather than on professional success in serving clients—this third error will undermine effective investment counseling.[7]

While the largest institutional clients with expert staffs are surely able to take on all their responsibilities without assistance from outside professionals, most investors—particularly individuals, but also investment committees at small and midsize public pension funds, corporate retirement funds, and the endowments of colleges, universities, museums, and hospitals—are understandably not experts on contemporary investing. Many want help working out the architecture of an optimal long-term investment program, and would appreciate having access to the best professional thinking and judgment.

Most investors can use professional help in developing a balanced, objective understanding of themselves and their situation: their investment knowledge and skills; their tolerance for risk in assets, incomes, and liquidity; their financial experiences and future needs; their financial resources; and their financial aspirations and obligations in the short and long run. Investors should know that the problem they most need to solve is *not* about beating the market. It is understanding the combination of those other factors that creates their own unique reality as investors and then working out the investment program best for them *and* then staying with it.

All investors are the same in that they all have many choices, their choices matter, and they all want to do well and avoid doing harm. At the same time, investors differ in assets, income, spending obligations and expectations, investment time horizons, investment skills, tolerance of risk and uncertainty, market experience, and financial responsibilities and obligations. With all these differences, it's no surprise that each investor is unique. So most can use help in designing investment programs that match their particular resources and specific objectives. This is the important work of investment counseling, almost always the most valuable professional service for almost all investors.

Done wisely, each investor can have a sensible investment program that, followed over the long term, has a high probability of success at both avoiding risks the investor cannot tolerate *and* success at achieving realistic long-term goals. This is a *winners' game*. Over a lifetime, the cumulative magnitude of such winning can be substantial.

The simplicity of indexing is its great power. It eliminates or reduces all the "little" things that, like termites, eat away at returns: high fees, costs of trading, costs of changing managers, taxes, errors in the selection of managers, and more. Research continues to show that the actions most investors take when trying to beat the market hurt far more than they help.

Indexing avoids almost all of the problems of operating in today's professionally dominant market, and investors get almost all the benefits of being part of our remarkable economy. Furthermore, indexing enables each of us to focus our time and attention on the really important questions such as: what are our core values, our present and future resources, and our realistic objectives? Answering these questions is far more important for long-term success than becoming expert traders, analysts, or portfolio managers.

Any individual or institution not yet ready to index would be wise to clarify the degree to which active investing has increased or reduced its own past returns. Most who look at their own records will see that they would have done better by indexing.

• • •

In Munich, while visiting my son and his wife one summer, we agreed to cheer for their friend who was running in a marathon. That friend had run several marathons and we had a realistic plan and knew that at about 11 o'clock, she would pass a particular church. So we were stationed there and, right on schedule, she came by. We cheered lustily; she waved and was quickly gone.

We went off to lunch at a wursthaus and then took the tram out to Munich's Olympic Park. As we walked from the tram station to the stadium and the marathon's finish line, we passed a trio of cheerful Kenyans who had already completed the race—probably coming in first, second, and third—and were going home. Our friend wouldn't finish the race for nearly an hour.

The organizers of the Munich Marathon had arranged an attractive way to finish. Runners would come into the stadium through a tunnel filled with a harmless gas cloud and then burst out into the sunlight as they entered the Olympic stadium with only one short lap around the stadium track left to go. The runners, nicely encouraged, loved it.

Sitting in the stadium with several hundred other fans, we enjoyed watching runners come through the portal entrance and into the stadium for their final lap to the finish line. They were different in age, dress, and running style, but in one particular way they were all the same: runner after runner, on entering the stadium, seeing the crowd, and hearing the scattered but friendly applause, reached high overhead with both arms in the traditional triumphal *V* for victory and held it for many seconds, grinning in triumph as they ran out the final lap.

At first, it seemed strange. Didn't they know the Kenyans had won long ago? As time went by—and we were there nearly two hours because our friend had caught a cramp and had to slow down—it might have seemed stranger and stranger to see later and later runners act like champions, heroes, and winners. Then it hit me: They *were* winners. They were *all* winners—because each runner had achieved her or his own realistic objective.

Some finished in less than three hours, some in only three hours, or "only" three and a half hours. Others beat their prior best time. Some won simply by completing the whole marathon, some for their first time and others for their last time. The powerful message: each runner had achieved his or her own realistic goal, so each *was* a true winner and fully entitled to make the big *V* and run the victory lap.

If, as investors, we would think and act the same way, understanding our capacities and our limits, we could plan the race that is right for us and, with the self-discipline of a long-distance runner, run our own race to achieve our own realistic goals. In investing, the good news is clear: *Everyone can win.* Everyone can be a winner. The secret to winning the winner's game in investing

The Index Revolution

is simple: Plan your play and play your plan to win *your* game.

My other favorite investing lesson came nearly 50 years ago. A freshly minted MBA, I was in a training program on Wall Street. As part of our training, we were to meet each Thursday for the hour before lunchtime with the heads of various departments—syndicate, trading, research, investment management, municipal bonds, and others—for an introductory explanation of each unit's work.

One day, we were happily surprised to learn that the senior partner had agreed to take a Thursday slot to discuss the larger picture. Joseph K. Klingenstein was known to his friends as Joe and to us as JK, except when he was or might be present, in which case he was always Mr. Klingenstein. He wore pince-nez glasses and was patrician, dignified, and erect.

As Mr. Klingenstein spoke about the history of his firm and of Wall Street and its traditions, we listened quietly but not, I fear, very conscientiously. Ten minutes before noon, Mr. Klingenstein had finished his talk and asked, "Do you young gentlemen have any questions?"

Silence.

The silence was broken by the brightest and certainly the most outspoken of our little group. "I've got a question for you, Mr. Klingenstein. You're rich. We all want to be rich, too, Mr. Klingenstein. So what can you tell us from all your experience, Mr. Klingenstein, about how to get rich like you, Mr. Klingenstein?"

We were mortified. Such a way to speak to such a very great man!

Joseph K. Klingenstein at first appeared angry. But then, to our great and collective relief, it became clear that he was silent because he was thinking very carefully about his many investment experiences. Finally, looking directly at his questioner, he said very simply and clearly, "Don't lose."

After JK rose and left the room, we all went off to lunch, where we agreed, "If you ask a silly question, you'll get a silly answer."

Many years have passed; Mr. Klingenstein's advice has come back to me again and again. Now, I know that in those two simple words, JK gave us the secret of investing successfully. While all the chatter and excitement is about big stocks, big gains, and "three-baggers," long-term investment success really depends on *not losing*—not taking major unnecessary losses.

Large losses are forever—in investing, in teenage driving, and in marital fidelity—and most big losses come from specific decisions to buy a particular stock or sell after a particular market decline or jump into a "hot" fund—trying to get too much and taking too much risk. If you avoid large losses with a strong defense, the winnings will have every opportunity to take care of themselves. Index funds, with their broad diversification, help protect us from overreacting to temptation and help us stay the course with our own long-term investment policies.

$$\bullet \quad \bullet \quad \bullet$$

Having explained the four major reasons for indexing in some detail, we now turn to a series of more modest additional reasons to index.

NOTES

1. In the United Kingdom, only two of the top 20 investment managers of 30 years ago continue to be leaders.
2. For example, Financial Engines and MarketRiders.
3. Managers of institutional funds often—surely, all too often—join in the deception by showing performance data to clients and prospects gross of fees, rather than net of fees. For many years, CFA Institute has advocated reform to address this issue.
4. John C. Bogle, *Don't Count on It!* (Hoboken, NJ: John Wiley & Sons, 2011), 74.

5. Terry Odean of the University of California, Los Angeles, has produced the best available data.

6. A. Goyle and S. Wahal, "The Selection and Termination of Investment Management Firms by Plan Sponsors," *Journal of Finance* 63, No. 4 (August 2008): 1805–1847. Of course, past performance had strongly favored the hired managers. One is left to wonder whether consultants who focus committee meetings on reviewing performance and on switching to "better" managers are really more interested in clients' long-term risk-adjusted returns or in convincing clients to continue paying their fees for service. Behavioral economists note that 80 percent of people rate themselves "above average" on many factors, including sense of humor, athletic ability, conversational skill, capacity for understanding others, parenting, and dancing.

7. One possible explanation of the shift away from counseling by investment managers is that, as they used more numerous and more specialized investment managers, pension fund executives wanted to separate the two functions and have independent investment consultants monitoring the managers just as outside auditors monitor financial reporting. Actually, integration of the two dimensions would be beneficial.

6

YOUR TAXES ARE LOWER WHEN YOU INDEX

Individual investors who index are able to avoid most of the taxes that must be paid by investors in actively managed mutual funds. Even if the investor holds on to the same mutual fund for the very long term, the typical active fund manager will have buy and sell turnover of 60 to 80 percent of the fund's portfolio each year, and some will have over 100 percent turnover. Some of those sales will, of course, be losses, but because the stock market is rising over the long term, more will be gains. Some of the gains will be long term and taxed at a capital gains rate and some will be short term and taxed at the investor's top rate for ordinary income. As a percentage of assets, the median active fund imposes an estimated 0.3 percent of assets more in tax costs on investors each year than the comparable index fund. That apparently small extra tax is, as shown in Chapter 4, seen correctly as 4 percent of expected average returns and much more as a percentage of incremental returns, if any, above indexing.

Index funds are different. And the difference is important. A typical index fund will have average annual turnover of only 5 to 10 percent of the portfolio as it adjusts to minor changes in the composition of the particular market index it is tracking. That means an average holding period of 10 to 20 years compared to 12 to 18 months in an actively managed mutual fund. Because index funds make these adjustments so seldom, almost none are short term. Nearly all are tax-favored capital gains. And because most index funds are growing and so are making add-on purchases, any redemptions can be accommodated without having to realize *any* gains.

Like fees and costs of operations, the higher taxes caused by active management are seldom noticed and almost never discussed. But over the long term, they add up: 4 percent of returns over 25 years equals an entire *year* of returns.

7

INDEXING SAVES OPERATIONAL COSTS

While investors seldom know or discuss the costs of portfolio operations, particularly the costs of trading, these invisible costs are real and reduce the investor's rate of return. Operational costs include all the costs of executing investment decisions, and are higher when an investment manager is buying when other funds are also buying the same stocks for much the same reasons. The same is true when your active manager and others are, for similar reasons, selling.

The reduction in returns due to the all-in transactions costs of active investing have been estimated at as much as 2 percent of assets per year. In a market and economic environment in which the generally expected rate of return is 7 percent, 2 percent would be nearly 30 percent of expected returns. And it may be lots of activity with little gain. What Paul Myners,[1] the respected British pension fund expert, aptly calls the "inertia index" shows, to the discomfort of active investors, that half the active managers would have achieved better results for most years if they had done nothing.

NOTES

1. Lord Myners led Gartmore Group during its best years as an active manager and wrote the much-admired "Myners Report."

8

INDEXING MAKES MOST INVESTMENT RISKS EASIER TO LIVE WITH

All investors must accept and learn to live with overall market risk. But we want to be smart about risk and develop our capacities to live with—not get "all shook up" by—the specific risks of individual stocks or particular industries. The best way to manage risk is to diversify. The more different stocks we own, the less we will worry about, be hurt by, or overreact to disappointment or "opportunity" in any particular stock or stocks in any one industry. Index funds, of course, own many different stocks in many different areas, which makes it easier to stay on plan for the long term.

When investors talk about risk, most are thinking about a particular stock falling unexpectedly. Falling stock prices are *not* the largest risk for most individual investors. A far larger risk can come with *rising* share prices—if they seduce us into getting overconfident and buying a stock that seems full of promise, only to learn later that we were way too hopeful as that stock dives in price, leaving us with a serious loss. A compounding risk can come when we overreact to that loss and then act too cautiously—sometimes for years. As we learn from behavioral economists, the great risk for most investors is inside ourselves, not in the stock market.

Any time an investor deviates from the market portfolio—a well-designed index fund—to be different, that investor is taking more risk to the extent of the difference. If you buy more small-cap stocks or more emerging-market stocks or more income stocks or more tech stocks or in any other way express your opinion that the market—the consensus of the experts—is wrong, you are taking the risk that *you* are wrong.

If you take money out of the market and hold it in cash, even though many would say you are being conservative, the reality is that you are taking on increasing risk—risk that the market will move up and you will miss part of the gain you could have had. The same is true if you tilt your portfolio to capture any underlying "theme" such as value or momentum. You may be correct, but you have to be right *twice*—once when you differentiate your portfolio from the total market and then again when you return to the market portfolio.

Taking risk doesn't necessarily mean you will lose or be wrong. But you will be different. And while active managers are always searching for creative and profitable ways to be different, their overall experience has not been favorable. It has been negative, as shown in the changing lists of Top 10 and Top 20 managers. Usually without knowing it, part-time investors who differ from the experts' consensus are taking large risks of making mistakes, mistakes that can be costly.

9

INDEXING AVOIDS "MANAGER RISK"

One of the negative realities that face clients of active managers is the real risk of unwelcome change in the portfolio manager—promotion to a different role at work, family troubles at home, aging, becoming less hungry or overconfident, and more. Other adverse changes may come within the manager's organization—large cash inflows that so often come with past success can make trading more costly (big block trades drive prices up) or oblige the manager to invest in larger, more liquid stocks; disputes over compensation or ownership or authority; changes in organizational structure; and more. Investment organizations are fragile *people* organizations, so changes can easily be destabilizing. The consequences of such risks can hurt investors' results.

Acquisitions of investment firms by larger organizations—often by insurance companies or giant banks headquartered in other countries—have been numerous. Few have had favorable consequences for the acquired outfit's investment clients. The acquirer has made a mainly *financial* decision to buy. So, of course, the new owner intends to achieve a good return on its capital investment by meeting or exceeding the earnings projections that were used to justify the purchase price. Hard business disciplines will dominate decisions, and soft professional priorities—creativity, interpersonal trust, accurate and timely communications, and careful attention to each client—are often the first to fade or go. As a consequence, profit-focused business managers, particularly if they have no particular reverence for the profession of investing, can report higher and higher bookkeeping profits while hollowing out an investment organization.

By the time clients become aware of the malaise, it may be too late to avoid significant slippage in performance.

Other causes of "deterioration in place" can come from a new sales manager who drives too hard for new business and accepts accounts that are not well suited to his firm's particular kind of investing. Or a new CEO who changes the culture and loses one or more inspirational professional investment leaders. Or new business piles up so fast that it overloads the capacities of the organization. Or individuals overly focus on their personal compensation and what they can take out rather than what they can contribute. Investment organizations and the key people within them can be fragile and require a special kind of nurturing. Any disruption can do real harm.

Another kind of problem—behavioral risk—arises when clients, both individuals and institutions, turn negative toward their active investment managers after a few years of underperformance and switch to managers with a recently favorable record. All too often, this positions these investors for another round of buy-high, sell-low dissatisfaction. For many investors, three straight years of underperformance would be too much to tolerate. A careful study of institutional hiring and firing, as already shown, reveals that, on average, the very managers fired for underperformance go on to outperform the newly hired managers. Another study found that most managers with superior long-term performance records had at some time experienced three or more consecutive years of significant underperformance.

As the evidence accumulates that clients hurt themselves and act against their own long-term interests, one conclusion is that a major benefit of indexing is that it is *not* interesting. The key to long-term success in investing has always been being rational with a persistent long-term focus. As the next chapter explains, indexing makes it much easier for investors to avoid getting distracted by Mr. Market.

10

INDEXING HELPS YOU AVOID COSTLY TROUBLES WITH MR. MARKET

Mistakes are costly. In investing, mistakes can be—and all too often are—both costly and *forever*. The most obvious and painful mistake comes when the stock market has gone down and down—and down again, causing investors to give up and sell out. This converts a short- or medium-term *market* loss that would be recovered when the market recovers into a *permanent* loss—a loss the investor will never recover. Another hurtful mistake is to get so intrigued by a hot stock that everyone is excited about that we buy in at peak prices, prices never to be seen again—and so suffer a serious loss. (Think of China in early 2015 or dot-com stocks at the millennium.)

Investors have two major "frenemies"—folks who appear to be friends but are really enemies of good results. One mischief maker, the source of many insights from the world of behavioral economics, is ourselves. And the other is Mr. Market. (I learned about Mr. Market from the great Benjamin Graham, the father of securities analysis, whose thinking I knew through reading his books and articles and, lucky me, from two three-day discussions of investment practices near his home in California.)

The stock market is fascinating *and* quite deceptive—in the short run. Over the very long run, the market can be almost boringly reliable and predictable. Understanding the personalities of two very different characters—Mr. Market and Mr. Value—is vital to a realistic understanding of the stock market and of yourself as an investor. Mr. Market gets all the attention because he's so interesting, while poor old Mr. Value goes about his important work almost totally ignored by investors. It's not fair! Mr. Value does all the work while Mr. Market has all the fun and causes all the trouble.

Mr. Market occasionally lets his enthusiasms *or* his fears run wild. Emotionally unstable, Mr. Market sometimes feels euphoric and sees only the favorable factors affecting a business. At other times he feels so depressed that he can see nothing but trouble ahead. To provoke us to action, he keeps changing his prices, sometimes quite rapidly. This most accommodating fellow stands ready, day after day, to buy if we want to sell or to sell if we want to buy. Totally unreliable and quite unpredictable, Mr. Market tries again and again to get us to do something— anything, but at least something. For him, the more activity, the better.

Mr. Market is a mischievous, but captivating fellow who persistently teases investors with all sorts of gimmicks and tricks such as surprising earnings reports, startling dividend announcements, sudden surges of inflation, inspiring presidential pronouncements, grim reports of commodities prices, announcements of amazing new technologies, ugly bankruptcies, and even threats of war. Just as magicians use clever deceptions to divert our attention, Mr. Market's short-term distractions can trick us and confuse our thinking about investments. Mr. Market dances before us without a care in the world. And why not? He has no responsibilities at all. As an economic gigolo, he has only one objective: to be attractive.

Meanwhile, Mr. Value, a remarkably stolid and consistent fellow, never shows—and seldom stimulates—any emotion. He lives in the cold, hard, real world where there is nary a thought about perceptions or feelings. He works all day and all night inventing, making, and distributing goods and services. His job is to grind it out on the shop floor, at the warehouse, in the computer lab, and the retail store—day after day, doing the *real* work of the economy. His role may not be emotionally exciting, but it sure is important.

Mr. Value always prevails in the long run. Eventually, Mr. Market's antics, like sand castles on the beach, come to naught. In the real world of business, goods and services are produced and distributed in much the same way and in much the same volume when Mr. Market is up as they are when he's down. Long-term investors need to avoid being shaken or distracted from their sound long-term policies for achieving favorable long-term results by Mr. Market and his constant jumping around. The daily changes in the market are no more important to a long-term investor than the daily weather is to a family deciding where to make their permanent home. Investors who wisely ignore the deceptive tricks of Mr. Market and pay little or no attention to current price changes can concentrate on real investment results over the long term.

Because it's always the surprising short-term events—mostly in specific stocks or companies—that Mr. Market uses to grab our attention, spark our emotions, and trick us into action, experienced investors study stock market history. The more we know about how securities markets have behaved in the past, the more we can understand their true nature and how they probably will behave in the future.

Investing is a continuous process like refining petroleum or manufacturing cookies, chemicals, or integrated circuits. If anything in the process is "interesting," it's almost surely wrong. That's why the biggest challenge for most investors is not intellectual; it's emotional—particularly with Mr. Market always trying to trick you into making changes. The hardest work is not figuring out the optimal investment policy. It's maintaining a long-term focus—particularly at market highs or market lows—and staying committed to an optimal investment policy.

Indexing helps investors avoid Mr. Market's tricks in several ways. With investments automatically made in several hundred stocks, investors don't get caught up in the details—no matter how fascinating or disturbing they might be if we paid too close attention to individual stocks. No single stock or group of stocks will become "too important" to us (which is why surgeons never operate on their own children). It's much easier to be rational when calm and much easier to be calm when dealing with an index fund holding 500 or more stocks.

Behavioral economists delight in showing us that not only are we humans not entirely rational (the core assumption of traditional economics), but also that our nonrational behavior can be measured and even predicted. Fortunately, we can use the insights of behavioral economists to understand ourselves (and our tendencies to err) so we can learn what mistakes to look out for and manage ourselves to be much more successful as investors.

Our worst mistakes in investing—as in so many parts of our lives—come when emotions override rationality and short-term behavior dominates long-term plans and intentions. Counting to 10 helps. Even better, ask yourself, "Will I really care 5 years from now?' Will I even remember 10 years from now?" Anything that helps you center on the long term and not get distracted by Mr. Market in the short run will help you act in your own best interests. Indexing helps a lot.

11

YOU HAVE MUCH BETTER THINGS TO DO WITH YOUR TIME

We would all like to have more time and more money. Given what we do have, economists never tire of encouraging us to appreciate that most of our decisions are trade-offs or allocations: time or money devoted to X must come from *not* spending time or money on Y.

If you can stop devoting time or money to investment operations, you can reallocate that free time as discussed in Chapter 5 to developing sound decisions on your all-important investment objectives and the sound investment policies most capable of your achieving success *and* developing your capacities to stay on policy through thick and thin. Indexing frees up time and energy previously spent on "buy and sell" decisions that are *not* helping. Now, you can redirect your time and energy to those much more important and productive major *policy* decisions. And that's not all.

You can also spend your time on noninvestment interests: extra time with your kids or reading books you haven't had time for or a new hobby—all better ways to use your precious, limited time.

12

EXPERTS AGREE MOST INVESTORS SHOULD INDEX

Each investor should make the decision to index independently and with careful reasoning, but it is important to recognize how consistently the leading experts in investing advocate indexing. Here are some experts speaking in favor of indexing:

"Most institutional and individual investors will find the best way to own common stock is through an index fund that charges minimal fees. Those following this path are sure to beat the net results [after fees and expenses] delivered by the great majority of investment professionals."[1]

—Warren Buffett, chairman of
Berkshire Hathaway

"A minuscule 4 percent of funds produce market-beating after-tax results with a scant 0.6 percent [annual] margin of gain. The 96 percent of funds that fail to meet or beat the Vanguard 500 Index Fund lose by a wealth-destroying margin of 4.8 percent per annum."[2]

"Unless an investor has access to incredibly highly qualified professionals, they should be 100 percent indexed. That includes almost all investors and most institutional investors."[3]

—David Swensen, chief investment
officer, Yale University

"Indexing makes sense because *indexing works*. It is the only strategy that effectively guarantees that investors will earn their fair share of whatever returns are provided by the stock and bonds markets.

> —John C. Bogle, founder and
> retired CEO of The Vanguard Group

"Index funds have regularly produced rates of return exceeding those of active managers by close to 2 percentage points. Active managers as a group cannot achieve gross returns exceeding the market as a whole and therefore must, on average, under-perform the indexes by the amount of their expense and transaction cost disadvantages."

> —Burton G. Malkiel, author of
> *A Random Walk Down Wall Street*

"In modern markets, most institutions and almost all individuals will experience better results with index funds."

> —Benjamin Graham, dean of
> the investment profession

"Most individual investors would be better off in an index mutual fund."[4]

> —Peter Lynch, legendary manager of
> the Fidelity Magellan Fund

"Forty years later [after the establishment of the first index fund], index funds remain the best wealth management choice for all investors."[5]

—Rex Sinquefield, cofounder of
Dimensional Fund Advisors

"People would be a lot more skeptical if they understood that there is an incredible amount of chance in the results that you observe for active managers. The distribution of outcomes is enormously wide—but that's exactly what you'd expect by chance with lots of active managers who hold imperfectly diversified portfolios. The really good portfolios contain a lot of really lucky picks, and the really bad portfolios contain a lot of really unlucky picks as well as some really bad ones."[6]

—Eugene Fama,
Nobel Laureate in Economics

"Investors shouldn't delude themselves about beating the market. They're just not going to do it. It's not going to happen."[7]

—Daniel Kahneman,
Nobel Laureate in Economics

"Even fans of actively managed funds often concede that most other investors would be better off in index funds. But buoyed by abundant self-confidence, these folks aren't about to give up on actively managed funds themselves. A tad delusional? I think so."[8]

—Paul Samuelson, Nobel Laureate
in Economics

"You will almost never find a fund manager who can repeatedly beat the market. It is better to invest in an index fund that promises a market return but with significantly lower fees."

—*The Economist*

"Those who have knowledge, don't predict. Those who predict, don't have knowledge."[9]

—Lao Tzu, 6th century B.C.

NOTES

1. Warren Buffett, Berkshire Hathaway Shareholder Letter, 1996.
2. David Swensen, quoted by John C. Bogle, *The Little Book on Common Sense Investing* (Hoboken, NJ: John Wiley & Sons, 2007).

3. Swensen quoted in news coverage from the *John C. Bogle Legacy Forum.*

4. *Barron's,* April 2, 1990, 15.

5. "40 Years Later, Index Funds Remain the Best Wealth Management Choice for All Investors," *Forbes.com,* September 5, 2013.

6. *Chicago Booth Magazine,* Fall 2013.

7. Daniel Kahneman, *Investors Can't Beat the Market,* 2002.

8. 2007

9. Lao Tzu, quoted by Bogle, *The Little Book of Common Sense Investing.*

APPENDIX A: HOW ABOUT "SMART BETA"?

Hopes that the increasing acceptance of indexing means investors are comfortably accepting the futility of striving to beat the market are now being challenged by a new phenomenon: so-called smart beta[1] broadly, that means indexing adjusted for factors other than market capitalization, such as momentum, dividends, value, volatility, or others. Hands down naming this *smart beta* has been a slick marketing winner—one of the best since the name *death* insurance was changed to *life* insurance. We know from the substantial market acceptance that smart beta has an almost magical appeal to investors who want to believe they can outperform an index. But what about the substance?

In the *Journal of Portfolio Management,* Princeton's Burton G. Malkiel, author of *A Random Walk Down Wall Street,* put the objective observer's view clearly when he concluded:

> ... *Many "smart beta" ETFs have failed to produce reliable excess returns, although a few have beaten the market over the [limited] lifetime of the funds. To the extent that some "smart beta" strategies have generated greater than market returns, those excess returns should be interpreted as a reward for assuming extra risk. In departing from the market portfolio, investors are taking on a different set of risks. "Smart beta" portfolios do not represent a sophisticated better mousetrap for investors. Investors should be wary of getting caught in the riskier mousetrap themselves. "Smart beta" fails the safety test.* ...[2]

Other disciplined observers have come to the same conclusion: there's not much there for most investors.

The basic idea, as always with new things in investing, is intuitively appealing and emotionally pleasing. We all know from history that markets go up and go down and that parts of the market go up and down somewhat differently. So wouldn't it be great to buy in when markets or segment of market—or factors that might drive segments—are low and then sell when markets or segments or factors are high, and then repeat, repeat, repeat? Unfortunately, past magical solutions—market timing, portfolio insurance, point-and-figure charting, technical analysis, portable alpha, and many more—have a long and consistent record of *failing*. So might it be much the same with "smart beta"?

If the manager is proficient at teasing the small increments of price advantage out of a rich, complex brew of minor and major forces that flow through securities markets, factors can work. Some factors are long wave, but most are short wave most of the time. Capturing benefits of the median and short-wave factors is like the now-disgraced old idea of market timing: the manager must be able to sense when to get on *and* when to get off a particular factor's favorable flow. (This can be more delicate than dry fly casting.)

We know the factors that seem most promising over the long term. Yet the record shows that none of these factors is *always* helpful. Each can be somewhat helpful fairly often and very helpful occasionally, but over the long term, they are unlikely to be always helpful to investors for two reasons: First, markets "learn" (because the investors who make the markets learn). If a factor works, investors will notice, move in on it, and reduce or even eliminate the real risk-adjusted advantage seen previously by earlier investors. In addition, a layer of fluctuating incremental returns will likely create a challenge on "factor timing": the rate-of-return record will look most attractive, particularly to less experienced investors at cyclical peaks. So enduring opportunities for superior risk-adjusted returns, whenever discovered, attract investors who "arbitrage" the opportunity away enough to make it insufficiently rewarding. Second, many factor anomalies are not enduring but cyclical, and gains driven by these factors reverse themselves and regress to the mean in rate of return. Hydrologists know the Gulf Stream always flows near the surface from the Caribbean toward England because it then doubles back under itself to recycle the water back to the Caribbean. But in the stock market, most factors that increase prices for a time cannot continue to increase prices, so the only possible destiny of a rising relative value is a subsequent decline or regression back to the mean. As the economist Herbert Stein famously said, "Any trend that cannot continue forever won't."

Since no driving factor will perpetually push prices higher, investors who want to exploit any of the well-known factors will need to judge successfully when to get aboard and when to get off—and when to get back on board again. (Morningstar thinks a better term than *smart beta* might be *strategic beta,* which at least acknowledges the need for active management—deciding when to move into the factors and when to move out.)

Factor-based or rule-based investing can work over the long term if either of two characteristics are demonstrated: (1) investors as a group are persistently biased or repeatedly make mistakes in ways that create persistent opportunity, or (2) a specific investor has an exploitable competitive advantage in information or understanding of factor-based investing. Operationally, investors trying to exploit the various factors need to be of sufficiently great skill and small scale in their activities that they don't change prices enough to offset the potential factor advantages.

If history repeats, too much money will overcrowd the cyclical opportunities as sales-minded securities firms create enough supply to flood the market with me-too products—usually after the best of times and all too often just before poor times for a particular strategy.

Any deviation from the expert consensus reflected in the market's prices is an active decision that the professionals who set those prices are wrong. Cyclical factor-based investing, like market timing, requires being right twice (or the market being wrong twice)—once when you climb aboard and once when you get off. So, except for a few experienced experts, it's not a reliable basis for long-term investing success. Furthermore, smart beta saddles investors with extra costs. (The average expense ratio of smart-beta exchange-traded funds [ETFs] is some 70 percent higher [0.41 percent versus 0.24 percent] than for traditional capitalization-weighted ETFs,[3] or $370 million in fees per year.) The number of skillful factor investors is small. The number of outfits that can package product and sell it to hopeful investors is, alas, large.

As is true with every other type of investing, success with factor investing requires well-developed skills—both on what to do (and when) and what not to do. Just as some active managers—but fewer and fewer—outperform the market averages, a few managers have shown unusual ability to capture factor advantages such as momentum and value, and a very few will continue to do so. Dimensional Fund Advisors, a fund manager, has done well at factor-based investing for many years with a disciplined, intellectually creative process and its panel of experienced academic experts. So has AQR. A few other firms might well succeed *if* left alone and free to make timely on-off-on decisions. But only a few.

But since most factor advantages are not perpetual—and cannot be—successful managers must have the skill and the discipline to emphasize and then deemphasize the propelling factors while they last and then move dexterously to another factor other managers have not yet seen. This is hard to do repeatedly. Investors should be appropriately skeptical and cautious.

Behavioral economists might suggest that smart-beta investors are seeing what they want to see. Objective investment experts would agree. We should try to pay more attention to Pogo's cautioning conclusion: "We have met the enemy and he is us."

NOTES

1. The term Smart Beta has been registered by Research Affiliates, which licenses its use for a fee.
2. Burton G. Malkiel, *Financial Analysts Journal*, Special 40th Anniversary Issue, 2014.
3. Denys Glushkov, Wharton Research Data Services, University of Pennsylvania, April 2015.

APPENDIX B: HOW TO GET STARTED WITH INDEXING

For those who choose active management, getting started means committing to a long series of detailed and often difficult decisions—some large, some small, many fraught with uncertainty and risk, and many coming at inconvenient times. By contrast, the basic indexing decisions are simple and, once made, stay decided until the time comes for a change in your long-term investment strategy because your goals have changed in an important way.

Well begun is half done, and making the decision to index *is* at least half of the task. The other half is deciding on the long-term portfolio mix (stocks vs. bonds and domestic vs. international) that will be best for you. (For many investors, this is a good time to retain the services of an experienced investment adviser.) Here are the steps to take next:

1. Select a major firm that is a leading index fund and ETF provider charging low fees and offering a range of index funds and ETFs. BlackRock, State Street Global, and Vanguard are the market leaders, and all meet the selection criteria. For index investors, the good news on pricing is that the major providers' already very low index fund fees continue to come down.

   Warning: Investors can still get charged *high* fees for index funds by managers that only dabble in indexing and somehow assume investors won't notice. So *caveat emptor!*

2. If you have an account with a stockbroker, buying index funds in that account is as easy as buying any stock. Your broker will do it for you. You may get some resistance because the broker knows that when an investor moves into

indexing, that investor won't be trading—and generating commissions for him.

If you don't have a Registered Investment Adviser or an account with a stockbroker, you can contact the index fund manager you choose by calling its 800 number or visiting its web site. Here are phone numbers for the Big Three: BlackRock, (800) 441-7762; State Street Global, (800) 997-7327; Vanguard, (800) 252-9578.

You are sure to be pleased with the capabilities of the service representative answering the phone and guiding you smoothly on implementation. Whether you are an absolute beginner or a seasoned indexer, the service representatives of these leading firms are highly trained and ready to help—and helping people feel comfortable is why they are there.

Most index investors will find everything involved in opening a new index fund account can be comfortably completed in much less than half an hour and you'll be on the right track, earning higher long-term returns at lower cost, for years to come.

3. Start by investing in a "plain vanilla" index fund of large and mid-sized company stocks like the S&P 500 (or the FTSE Index) or a total market fund that includes smaller companies. All indexes—and, therefore, all index funds—are dominated by the leading companies.

4. Your next decision is whether to combine your "domestic" index fund with an "international" index fund. (The use of quotes is a reminder that many "domestic" companies like Coca-Cola earn a majority of their profits in international markets. And some "international" companies—like BP—earn most of *their* profits in the United States.)

About half of the global stock market is U.S. "domestic" and about half is "international," so if you want maximum diversification, you'll go 50-50. Markets go up and down differently, so perhaps once a year you may want to rebalance back to your original index portfolio structure. If you use a global index fund (combining both U.S. and international markets), no rebalancing is called for: it's done for you.

5. If you prefer less international diversification, limit international to 10 percent or 20 percent or 30 percent—whatever feels comfortable to you. (Investors based in New Zealand or Spain or Canada should be comfortable investing more than half of their investments outside their smaller home markets.)

6. Because one of the great benefits of indexing is that it implements your long-term investment policy decisions so effectively, be sure to make only those commitments you plan to stay with for the long term—10 years or longer. This is savvy self-discipline on your thinking. (You can always change your holdings whenever you have good long-term reason to change your investment policy.)

7. Next, you'll want to decide on the right percentages for you of stocks versus bonds—just as you would decide if you were still an active investor. (Note that most investors limit their thoughts to stocks and bonds, ignoring such assets as a home, future Social Security benefits, and, most particularly, the net present value of

future earnings at work—for young professionals, by far their largest asset. If you take a "whole picture" view of all your assets—as we all should—you'll be less concerned about Mr. Market's moves in just the securities portion of your total portfolio and, almost certainly, will invest less in bonds because home, future income, and future Social Security benefits can all be thought of as close to stable value fixed-income equivalents.)

8. One high-grade bond index fund and one index equity fund—either domestic or global—in the proportions that are right for you will provide you with a widely diversified, low-cost portfolio that will outperform most active funds with less risk and lower taxes *and* provide more confidence and comfort *and* take less time.

9. After experience with the basic index funds, you may decide you strongly expect superior long-term prospects for a particular kind of investment or nation—emerging-market stocks or small-cap stocks or Japanese stocks,

for example—that you want to emphasize or "overweight." Again, don't ever do anything you do not intend to stay with for at least a decade because indexing works best when sustained long term.

APPENDIX C: HOW INDEX FUNDS ARE MANAGED

First came indexes to track the overall stock market. (The first index, the Dow Jones Industrial Average, originally created in 1896 by Charles Dow, had only 12 stocks, weighted not by their total capitalization, but by the prices of 12 single stocks.) Then came index funds that matched the indexes with small amounts of invested money. Then, after a slow start, larger and larger amounts of money began to flow into index funds and into exchange-traded funds (ETFs). Today, thousands of stock, bond, and commodities index funds and ETFs cover every market and all sorts of submarkets.

Anyone can create an index, but most indexes are produced by a small group of firms that develop indexes and charge index fund managers a licensing fee. Standard & Poor's, or S&P, is now combined with Dow Jones indexes. FTSE, which originated as the *Financial Times'* joint venture with the London Stock Exchange, now includes the Frank Russell series of indexes. MSCI began as the Capital International group of stock indexes and was acquired by Morgan Stanley.

While many index investors correctly assume that indexes and the index funds that replicate them are stable, managers of index funds correctly focus on such details as how to define growth and value stock indexes. The two are not separated by a bright line, and stocks do move from one index to another. The same is true for large-cap versus mid-cap versus small-cap versus micro-cap stocks. A pure "rules-based" approach that has total transparency precludes arguments over specific stocks being included or not included. But a more subjective approach may result in fewer and more orderly changes. (Index fund managers usually favor weighting by the number of shares that are available to public investors, or "float," and so would exclude holdings by other corporations or insiders.)

If index fund managers were to adhere to narrow, rigid boundaries, portfolio turnover and costs would rise as stocks moved back and forth across the boundaries. To avoid this cost, index fund managers advocate using bands, not bright lines, as the boundaries. Index fund managers sometimes change the indexes they track to save costs of licensing the index they use or to use a "more perfect" index that better reflects market realities. Gus Sauter, for 25 years Vanguard's lead manager of index funds, advocates not only boundary bands, but also implementing one-twelfth of a year's change each month to minimize market impact and cost of execution. Sauter also maintains that terms like *growth* and *value* are not determined by portfolio theory but should reflect the way investment managers actually think and work.

ABOUT THE AUTHOR

Charles D. Ellis is a consultant to large public and private institutional investors, and leading sovereign wealth funds. For three decades he was managing partner of Greenwich Associates, the international business strategy consulting firm. He serves as chair of Whitehead Institute, and on the investment committee for King Abdullah University in Saudi Arabia, was a director of Vanguard, chair of Yale's investment committee and trustee of the university, and as a trustee and chair of the finance committee at the Robert Wood Johnson Foundation. One of 12 individuals cited for lifetime leadership in investments, has taught the advance investment courses at both Harvard Business School and Yale School of Management, and is the author of 17 books, including the best-selling *Winning the Loser's Game.*

INDEX